S£6.50

PERGAMON INTERNATIONAL LIBRARY
of Science, Technology, Engineering and Social Studies
The 1000-volume original paperback library in aid of education,
industrial training and the enjoyment of leisure
Publisher: Robert Maxwell, M.C.

European Social Policy, Today and Tomorrow

THE PERGAMON TEXTBOOK
INSPECTION COPY SERVICE

An inspection copy of any book published in the Pergamon International Library will gladly be
sent to academic staff without obligation for their consideration for course adoption or
recommendation. Copies may be retained for a period of 60 days from receipt and returned if not
suitable. When a particular title is adopted or recommended for adoption for class use and the
recommendation results in a sale or 12 or more copies, the inspection copy may be retained with
our compliments. The Publishers will be pleased to receive suggestions for revised editions and
new titles to be published in this important International Library.

European Social Policy, Today and Tomorrow

BY

MICHAEL SHANKS

PERGAMON PRESS

OXFORD   •   NEW YORK   •   TORONTO   •   SYDNEY
PARIS   •   FRANKFURT

U. K.	Pergamon Press Ltd., Headington Hill Hall, Oxford OX3 0BW, England
U. S. A.	Pergamon Press Inc., Maxwell House, Fairview Park, Elmsford, New York 10523, U.S.A.
C A N A D A	Pergamon of Canada Ltd., 75 The East Mall, Toronto, Ontario, Canada.
A U S T R A L I A	Pergamon Press (Aust.) Pty. Ltd., 19a Boundary Street, Rushcutters Bay, N.S.W. 2011, Australia
F R A N C E	Pergamon Press SARL, 24 rue des Ecoles, 75240 Paris, Cedex 05, France
W E S T G E R M A N Y	Pergamon Press GmbH, 6242 Kronberg-Taunus, Pferdstrasse 1, West Germany

First edition 1977

Library of Congress Cataloging in Publication Data
Shanks, Michael, 1927 -
European social policy, today and tomorrow

1. European Economic Community — Social policy.
2. European Economic Community — Economic policy.
I. Title.
HN380.5.A8S52 1977   309.1'4   77-4245
ISBN 0-08-021444-4 (Hardcover)
ISBN 0-08-021443-6 (Flexicover)

Printed in Great Britain by Biddles Ltd., Guildford, Surrey

Contents

Preface

The "Europe" of this book is primarily the nine-nation Europe of the European Community or E.E.C.[1] The perspective from which it is written is that of the central institutions of the Community and their interface with national policies and institutions. But the Community is not a self-contained world, and any examination of its policies has to consider also trends and developments in the neighbouring countries. Moreover, an examination of E.E.C. social policy which dealt only at Community level and failed to examine the very diverse trends and patterns within the individual member-States would be sterile and academic. I hope I have avoided this pitfall in this study.

My main personal qualification for writing this book is that between May 1973 and January 1976 I served as director-general for social affairs in the European Community in Brussels — a period characterised by an English expert as "the time when the Community not only acquired a wide-ranging social policy but made it visible and felt".[2] But it was also a period during which the process of European integration started by the Treaties of Paris and Rome came under severe strain, and when the economies of the member-States were reeling under the impact of unemployment and inflation. I believe, and it is my main motive in writing this book to establish and elaborate, that if the European Community is to survive and prosper in the years ahead it must develop a viable social policy which is seen to relate to the problems and priorities confronting the man and woman in the street, and in which the relative roles of the Community and the individual member-States are clearly defined. If this

---

1 These are: Belgium, Denmark, France, West Germany, Ireland, Italy, Luxembourg, Netherlands, United Kingdom.

2 Michael Fogarty, *Work and Industrial Relations in the European Community*, Chatham House/P.E.P., May 1975.

message does not emerge clearly from the chapters ahead, I will have failed in my task.

The term "social policy" is not yet a very familiar one to an Anglo-Saxon audience. I define it in this book pragmatically as being essentially the work carried out by the directorate-general of social affairs in the European Commission. This corresponds to the activities embraced by the following British Departments of State: Employment, Health and Social Security, Housing, Education (considered as a social service), Home Office (in so far as it relates to the rights of the citizen), Environment (as concerns its interest in urban and anti-pollution problems). The scope for Community as opposed to national policies in this area varies from sector to sector, and this is one of the themes pursued in this book.

It will be obvious that in acquiring the experience which enabled me, however inadequately, to undertake this task, I owe a debt of gratitude to my former colleagues in the services of the Commission which I cannot hope to discharge. It would be invidious to mention any of them individually, and I will not do so — especially as doing so might appear to saddle them with the responsibility for the many errors of fact and interpretation which no doubt remain in my text, and for which of course I alone am responsible. But I hope that if any of them read this book they will not feel that I have distorted matters too grossly. This is an area of great complexity and, I believe, of great importance for the survival of our civilisation. In a land as yet almost devoid of maps, even a rough sketch may be better than nothing.

Little Kingshill,
 England
 October 1976

Technical Note

To avoid cluttering the ensuing text with footnotes it might be useful before beginning this book to describe briefly the institutions and functioning of the European Community and some of the technical terms in use in it.

The main institutions of the European Economic Community, or *E.E.C.*, are:

(1) The *Commission*, which is the executive body, headed by thirteen Commissioners, charged with making recommendations for European integration in conformity with the *Treaty of Rome*.

(2) The *Council of Ministers*, representing the nine (formerly six) member-governments (sometimes called the Nine or the Six), which has the responsibility of deciding on proposals from the Commission.

(3) The *European Parliament* and the *Economic and Social Committee* (Ecosoc), which are purely consultative bodies, charged with advising the Council of Ministers on the actions it should take with regard to Commission proposals.

(4) The *European Court of Justice*, the supreme judicial organ of the Community, which does not appear in this text.

Merged in the E.E.C., but formerly separate, are the *European Coal and Steel Community* (E.C.S.C.) established by the *Treaty of Paris* (its executive body, corresponding to the Commission, was called the *High Authority*), and *Euratom*, set up to administer the nuclear power industries of the Six (now the Nine).

Commission proposals normally take three alternative forms:

(1) *Regulations,* if agreed by the Council, automatically are embodied

in national legislation in member-countries; more common are:
(2) *Directives.* Here, if accepted by the Council, member-governments are obliged to adopt the principles in national legislation, but there can be some flexibility in the detailed application to suit differing national circumstances.
(3) *Recommendations,* which have no legal force.

The Treaty of Rome established, as the first stage of integration among the Six, a *common market,* in which in principle there was free movement of goods, people and capital. The phrase is sometimes loosely and erroneously used as a synonym for the E.E.C. In this book it is used only in its strict technical sense.

Some other abbreviations used in the book are:

EMU. Economic and Monetary Union (explained in text).
Social Partners. Employer and trade union organisations.
Comecon. The economic bloc consisting of the U.S.S.R. and the East European Soviet bloc countries (as well as some non-European Communist states, such as Cuba and Outer Mongolia).
O.E.C.D. The Organisation for Economic Cooperation and Development, an inter-governmental body including the U.S.A., the main Western European countries and some others.

Practically all the documents of the Commission referred to in the text (including the social action programme but *not* the Social Budget) are available from the Commission's information offices, which are located in the capitals of each of the Nine, and also in Washington, Tokyo and Geneva. The full title of the "Green Paper" referred to in Chapter 5 is "Green Paper on Employee Participation and Company Structure in the European Communities", published in November 1975. The title of the Sudreau Report, mentioned in the same chapter, is *La Reforme de l'Entreprise,* published by the French Government in February 1975.

The Commission publishes annually a General Report on its activities, and also an annual *Report on the Development of the Social Situation,* which contains a wealth of useful information both about the Community and individual member-countries.

There is a serious lack of books about E.E.C. social policy as such in the English language, though there are some very useful comparative studies on certain aspects of social policy. Among these might be mentioned:

Job Power by David Jenkins (Heinemann).

Trade Unions in Europe by Margaret Stewart (Employment Conditions Abroad/Gower).

Prelude to Harmony on a Community Theme: Health Care Insurance Policies in the Six and Britain by Jozef van Langendonck (Oxford University Press).

Europe and the British Health Service by Lord Wade (National Council of Social Service).

Through No Fault of their Own: Systems for Handling Redundancies in Britain, France and Germany by Santosh Mukherjee (Macdonald).

Governments and Labour Markets: Aspects of Policies by Santosh Mukherjee (P.E.P.).

Free Trade is Good, but what about the Workers? by Santosh Mukherjee (P.E.P.).

Economic and Monetary Integration in Europe, ed. Geoffrey Denton (Croom Helm, for Federal Trust) .

There are also a number of pamphlets and studies on aspects of the subject published by the Royal Institute for International Affairs, P.E.P. and Federal Trust. But there is room for more such studies of book length, particularly in such fields as public health policy, migration, social protection, personal social services, labour law and industrial relations, worker participation, wage determination and labour market policy.

One final point. This book tries to provide a snapshot of E.E.C. social policy at a particular moment of time, towards the end of 1976. As it is being written, the Commission is coming to the end of the three-year social action programme described in this book, and is preparing its successor, which will probably have been presented to the Council of Ministers by the time this book appears. This is the perennial hazard faced by authors writing about current events. However, it seems unlikely that the basic lineaments of the situation will have changed significantly, and the basic lessons of the book, if they have any validity at the time of writing, will certainly not have lost it by the time of publication.

CHAPTER 1

European Integration and Social Policy

Social policy played a rather unimportant role in the stages of European integration up to and including the Treaty of Rome (1957). It is true that the Treaty pays lip service in several passages to the need for social as well as economic progress, but the actual clauses dealing with specific social issues are relatively few. The reason for this is clear. At the time when the Treaty was signed, the dominating philosophy in Western Europe was one of *laisser-faire*. The unspoken assumption underlying the Treaty is that, if only the artificial barriers obstructing the free movement of labour, capital and goods can be removed, so that all enterprises throughout the Community compete on equal terms, this in itself will ensure the optimum distribution of resources, the optimum rate of economic growth and thus the optimum social development of the European Community. Thus there was little need to write specific social provisions into the Treaty.

In fact the earlier Treaty of Paris (1951) which set up the European Coal and Steel Community (E.C.S.C.) had rather more to say about social policy. This is not surprising, since that Treaty, unlike the later Rome Treaty, had to concern itself with major issues of rationalisation in two key problem industries. It was therefore perforce more interventionist in tone, and it could hardly avoid concerning itself with the social impact of structural changes in its industries. Thus Article 3 of the Paris Treaty stated the purpose of the institutions of the Community as being "to promote improved working conditions and an improved standard of living for the workers in each of the industries for which it is responsible". The Treaty gave the E.C.S.C. High Authority powers to finance substantial resettlement schemes, including free occupational training, and also research into industrial hazards and diseases (Articles 55 and 56). From 1954 to the end of 1971 some $333 million had been spent, 50% by the High Authority and 50% by member-governments of the Six, to help 440,000 displaced coal and steel workers find new jobs. In the same period the E.C.S.C. helped to finance research programmes into industrial hazards and diseases such as silicosis, bronchitis, gas poisoning and mine dust, and on accident statistics. In 1956 the E.C.S.C. set up a permanent Committee on Mine Safety, with members drawn from governments, employers and unions, to study and make recommendations on ways of reducing pit hazards. Later a similar committee was established for the steel industry, though in this case membership consisted only of unions and employers and did not include governments. Also, the E.C.S.C. High Authority had a specific remit to help mobility by assisting in the finance of housing for coal and steel workers. By the end of 1974 more than 130,000 such houses had been financed by low-interest E.C.S.C. loans for renting or owner-occupation.

The European Commission, set up to implement the Rome Treaty, did not have the same sponsorship functions as the E.C.S.C. High Authority, so it is not surprising that the social element should be even less intrusive. When the three European Communities (the E.E.C., E.C.S.C. and Euratom) were merged in the late 1960s — a merger which in effect constituted a takeover of the two smaller Communities by the E.E.C. — the now single Community took over from the defunct E.C.S.C. High Authority its responsibilities for health and safety, housing and vocational training, as well as taking over from Euratom its "social" responsibilities for ensuring the safety of nuclear power stations and their emissions. But initially these responsibilities remained limited to their original industries. At that stage there was no attempt to extend work on housing, health and safety or pollution control to the wider industrial field covered by the Treaty of Rome. There was, in any case, a major difference in budgeting between the E.C.S.C., on the one hand, and the other two Communities, on the other. The E.C.S.C. was partly financed by a levy on coal and steel enterprises. The "social" activities of the E.C.S.C. — particularly its work on health and safety research — were seen partly as a return for the levy. Since the levy remained after the merger of the Communities, it seemed only fair that the two contributing industries should get something special in return for their money. So the E.C.S.C. social programmes remained largely separate from the work of the E.E.C., financed as they were by a separate budget (and located, as they continued to be after the merger, in Luxembourg rather than Brussels; this was also true of the Euratom activities).

The situation was different in that part of E.C.S.C. work devoted to the promotion of mobility through stimulating and financing vocational training. In this field the E.E.C. set up early in its life the European Social Fund with the purpose of assisting mobility out of declining areas of the economy by providing grants for vocational training and resettlement on a fifty-fifty basis with member-governments — exactly as under Article 56 of the E.C.S.C. Treaty. This was the one case in which an E.C.S.C. social activity was taken up by the E.E.C.; and in due course the work of Article 56 was in effect to be absorbed in the Social Fund.

But, important as it was to be as a harbinger of things to come, until the 1970s the Social Fund operated on a very small scale, and its role in overall Community policy was minor. The same could be said for the whole field of social policy in the Community structure during the 1960s. It was only at the very end of the decade that the need for a more active and ambitious social element in the integration process began to be felt.

The Birth of a Social Policy

By the end of the 1960s a new spirit was abroad in Europe. The Common Market had been in operation for more than a decade, and it had brought with it, as its protagonists had claimed, an economic boom of unprecedented dimensions. The average European was enjoying a standard of living hitherto undreamed of, and as wealth grew horizons widened and expectations burgeoned.

The results were, however, not always reassuring. Growth had been bought at a price, and the readiness of the average European to pay that price was visibly diminishing. There was a growing awareness, first, of the *unevenness* of growth. The expansion in jobs had taken place primarily in the central areas of the Community. The peripheral areas — south-west France, West Berlin, above all the *Mezzogiorno* of southern Italy — were losing ground and lagging increasingly in economic development behind the richer areas. The unevenness of development was not just a regional phenomenon, however. Within the labour market, certain groups were having difficulty in securing a reasonable share of jobs. Such groups included the *handicapped,* whose problems of rehabilitation were severe; *women*, guaranteed equality of pay with men for equivalent work under Article 119 of the Rome Treaty but in fact encountering various obstacles in the labour market which they were increasingly unready to accept; and certain categories of *young* and *old* workers. There were also the *migrant* workers, brought into the boom centres of the Common Market not only from southern Italy but also from non-Community countries such as Turkey, Greece, Spain, Portugal, Jugoslavia and the Maghreb countries of North Africa: workers who formed in general the lowest level of labour in the Community, accepted as workers but not as citizens, with growing problems of social integration and discrimination.

So the unevenness of economic development was posing problems for the under-privileged regions and the under-privileged sections of the work force. But, perhaps more serious, there was also a growing intolerance of some of the *costs* of economic growth. There was increasing concern about the effects on the environment of industrial *pollution*. There was growing concern about standards of health and safety in various sectors of industry and about the poor quality of working life in many factories — the absence of job security and industrial democracy, the boring and repetitive nature of many jobs, the lack of participation. All of these were acceptable when Europe was poor as the necessary price to be paid for growth. But now Europe had become rich they were less acceptable.

Above all, perhaps, what Europeans were questioning was the pace of change which the boom had generated. During the 1960s three simultaneous revolutions were in progress throughout the European Community. There was, first, the *agricultural* revolution as the Community moved away from a peasant economy to a more capital-intensive agriculture which no longer needed so many people to produce food; throughout this period there was a steady movement of workers out of agriculture into industry and the service sector. Second, there was a *technological* revolution as the industries of Europe began to narrow the technological gap *vis-à-vis* American industry. Third, and perhaps most important of all, there was a *structural* revolution brought about by the Common Market itself, with the elimination of tariff and trade barriers between the member-States leading to the disappearance of major sectors and enterprises which had previously enjoyed protected markets, and the expansion of others to take advantage of the emerging international market of the Community. All of these changes brought added wealth to the Community as a whole; but they did so at the cost of massive and continual changes for individuals, in their place of work, the nature of their work, the skills and attributes required. As the 1960s drew to a close and people came to take the fruits of growth increasingly for granted, the tolerance of change began visibly to diminish. Some people, in the European Community as elsewhere, argued that the costs of growth had come to outweigh its benefits. In the early 1970s Sicco Mansholt, the Dutch President of the Commission, tried to persuade his colleagues to espouse a "no-growth" policy. He did not succeed — but even those who continued to press the need for growth were forced to recognise that it could no longer continue on the *laisser-faire* principles of the Treaty of Rome without risking major social and political frictions. In short, if the process of economic growth was to continue to be socially and politically acceptable, it must be accompanied — and be seen to be accompanied — by an active programme of social reform designed to humanise the process of change and to spread the fruits of growth more equitably.

Similarly, there was a political need to involve the trade unions and their members more actively in the work of European integration. The unions were increasingly complaining that they had not been allowed to inject their own thinking sufficiently into the "making of Europe", so that the Europe that was emerging was not one with which they could identify and which would command their loyalty. European politicians from the Social Democratic stable — above all Chancellor Willy Brandt of West Germany — were very conscious of the need to harness the support of the labour movement to Europe by giving the Community more political appeal — more of a "human face", as the jargon of the day had it.

This was especially urgent as the Community was in a sense starting to run out of steam. The elimination of barriers to the free movement of resources — in other words the establishment of the Common Market — had been largely achieved. Where barriers still existed — as, for example, in the refusal to accept the validity of diplomas from other Community countries which restricted the freedom of professional people to practise their skills abroad — there were stubborn political or institutional reasons which could not easily be disposed of. The common agricultural policy was in being. The original mandate of the Rome Treaty had been largely carried out. But the process envisaged by the original founders of the Community, whereby the creation of a Common Market would in itself generate irresistible pressures for further integration leading eventually to a United States of Europe, was not taking place. The momentum of European integration seemed to be slowing down. So a new set of priorities was needed to provide the momentum for a further great leap forward to a future united Europe.

So, during the early years of the 1970s much thought was being given to a new "package" — a series of measures which would, on the one hand, accelerate the process of integration and at the same time deepen and broaden the concept of "Europe" from a trading-cum-economic bloc to a Community expressing real social values; a package which would find ways of compensating those who were in any way adversely affected by the integration process. Thinking about this European "new deal" was going on simultaneously with the crucial negotiations to enlarge the Community, which culminated in the accession of the United Kingdom, Ireland and Denmark in the autumn of 1972. The Six had become the Nine, and in the process the social dimensions of the Community had become different and considerably more complex.

At the end of 1972, at the successful completion of the negotiations for an enlarged Community, the heads of government of the nine member-States met in Paris to chart the future course of the new Community of the Nine. It was a moment of euphoria. Not only had the enlargement negotiations succeeded; the three most powerful leaders in the Community — Chancellor Brandt of Germany, President Pompidou of France, Prime Minister Edward Heath of the United Kingdom — had established a remarkable personal rapport, and each appeared to be in a strong domestic position, so that each was prepared to think deeply about the future of Europe and to accept commitments which in more stressful times they would have resisted. It was to be the last such moment for several years.

The summit meeting endorsed a "new deal" for the Community which contained the following main features:

(1) The next main stage of integration would be through the establishment of Economic and Monetary Union (the so-called "snake in the tunnel"), under which member-States would align their currencies as a first step towards full-scale economic and monetary integration; because of their economic weakness, as a temporary measure Italy, the U.K. and Ireland would delay entry into the E.M.U., but there was general understanding that this delay would be brief.

(2) Since it was recognised — and indeed this was one of its purposes —

that the E.M.U. would impose strict disciplines on the member-States, and that these would bear hardest on the weakest countries and regions, which tended to be those on the periphery of the Community, a European Regional Development Fund would be set up to help to establish a more even rate of growth throughout the Community by financing investment in the poorer regions. This fund, like the European Social Fund, would be financed by the member-States according to their wealth — in other words, the main financiers would be Germany and France.

(3) The Community would coordinate its economic policy *vis-à-vis* third countries, including its overseas aid policy which would be expanded.

(4) The Community should develop active programmes of social reform, environmental and consumer protection in order to broaden its appeal and improve the quality of life in all member-States. The heads of government stressed that they would attach as much importance to vigorous action in the social field as to the achievement of economic and monetary union, and they called on the Community institutions to draw up a social action programme focused on the three broad objectives of:

(a)　full and better employment;
(b)　the improvement of living and working conditions;
(c)　the increased involvement of management and labour in the economic and social decisions of the Community and of workers in the life of undertakings.

They also stressed the importance in this general context of the expanded European Social Fund which had been reformed and greatly strengthened in 1971.

It is not hard to discern the strategy behind the "new deal". On the one hand, a balance is struck between the strong and the weak. Further economic integration via economic and monetary union creates risks for the weaker sections which are to be defused by use of the Regional and Social Funds. At the same time, social and political objections to integration are met by the development of active Community policies in areas of general concern (social, environmental, consumer protection — and in a rather different category, overseas aid) where the Treaty of Rome was largely silent. It was in a very real sense a "package deal" which contained in the best Community tradition something for everybody.

It had, however, one very great flaw. Because it had no sanction in the

Treaty, the force of the mandate given to the Community institutions (primarily the Commission) to prepare new measures in these areas depended entirely on the political will of the nine member-States. In Community parlance, the juridical basis was weak. Unfortunately the political will which could have compensated for this, and which was very strong at the time of the summit conference, evaporated with alarming speed during 1973 and 1974.

Partly this was a matter of personalities. The presiding geniuses of the conference were Brandt, Heath and Pompidou. Pompidou died; Heath lost office; Brandt resigned. There were changes at the top in all the other six countries too. Those who had a personal commitment to the summit communiqué and the ''new deal'' which it enunciated tended to disappear from the political scene during 1973 and 1974.

They and their successors had in any case other worries to preoccupy them during this period. Inflation accelerated during 1973, fuelled by the oil crisis which followed the Yom Kippur war between Israel, Egypt and Syria, and the resulting explosion in oil prices. Every country in Western Europe found itself facing masssive problems in its balance of payments (though some were to achieve a payments turnround much faster than others), and a desperate need to contain public spending. In 1974 the long boom ended, and Europe experienced the unprecedented combination of unemployment and inflation. The Community was facing its worst economic crisis since its inception, and, as in other economic crises, the stability and self-confidence of national governments weakened. In these circumstances it is not surprising that the political will to strengthen the Community, which was so evident at the end of 1972, proved an early casualty of the crisis.

Nevertheless, during 1973 the European Commission pressed forward, as instructed by the summit, with programmes for social reform, regional development, environmental and consumer protection, worker participation, and overseas aid. The proposals for social reform were enshrined in the so-called Social Action Programme, which was in fact approved by the European Council of Ministers in January 1974. In the next chapter we will describe this programme and the fate of its main measures and indicate more briefly the progress in other areas of the ''new deal''. In the subsequent chapters we will assess the situation in particular sectors in more detail before turning in the concluding chapters to the main issues still unresolved, and suggesting a way forward out of the dilemma in which the Community finds itself in 1976. But the issue which we will be confronting throughout, in its various manifestations, is that posed in this first chapter. Can European integration be achieved on the relatively narrow *laisser-faire* basis set out in the Treaty of Rome? If not, what more is needed? And can that extra element, whatever it is, be meaningfully pursued by a European Community structured as ours is today — in other words, can political will adequately supplement the Treaty or supplant it? Or — to put the same question in a slightly different way — does the European Community have a role to play in the social field (broadly defined to include the other "human face" or "quality of life" fields) over and above that of its member-States? If so, what is it? If not, what is the degree of social diversity (again, broadly defined) which the European Community can tolerate and survive? If, when stated baldly like this, these questions have a somewhat gnomic character, hopefully the ensuing chapters will help to elucidate (if not to solve) them.

CHAPTER 2

European Social Policy Today

The social action programme approved by the Council of Ministers in January 1974 reflected the results of an intensive process of preparation and consultation carried out by the Commission since 1971. In response to the rather general mandate of the summit conference some 15 months before, it was a somewhat disparate package of measures covering a very broad canvas; the tone was pragmatic rather than ideological. The programme contained some three dozen individual proposals to be implemented over the ensuing three years. Some of these — such as commitments to improve statistics on various aspects of social policy — were essentially internal measures under the control of the Commission. But about half were important political proposals requiring the assent of the member-States. Under the terms of the Council resolution approving the programme, the Commission undertook to bring forward each of these proposals separately over the following three years and get the approval of the Council individually for each item. So the approval given to the programme as a whole in January 1974 was a "concept approval" only. All the individual items in the package had to be produced and argued through the Council separately.

The priority items listed in the programme were as follows:

Full and Better Employment

(1) The establishment of appropriate consultation between member-States on their employment policies and the promotion of better cooperation by national employment services;
(2) The establishment of an action programme for migrant workers who are nationals of member-States or third countries;
(3) The implementation of a common vocational training policy and

the setting up of a European Vocational Training Centre;

(4) The undertaking of action to achieve equality between men and women as regards access to employment and vocational training and advancement and as regards working conditions, including pay.

Improvement of Living and Working Conditions

(1) The establishment of appropriate consultations between member-States on their social protection policies;

(2) The establishment of an initial action programme, relating in particular to health and safety at work, the health of workers and improved organisation of tasks, beginning in those economic sectors where working conditions appear to be the most difficult;

(3) The implementation, in cooperation with the member-States, of specific measures to combat poverty by drawing up pilot schemes.

Participation

(1) The progressive involvement of workers or their representatives in the life of undertakings in the Community;

(2) The promotion of the involvement of management and labour in the economic and social decisions of the Community.

In addition to these nine priority items, there was a further group of measures to which the Commission itself attached a special priority, partly because the detailed measures could be prepared relatively quickly:

(1) Assistance from the European Social Fund for migrant workers and for handicapped workers.

(2) An action programme for handicapped workers in an open market economy.

(3) The setting up of a European General Industrial Safety committee and the extension of the competence of the Committee on Mine Safety to cover other extractive industries.

(4) A directive on the approximation of member-States' legislation on collective dismissals.

(5) A directive on the harmonisation of laws with regard to the retention of workers' rights and advantages in the event of changes in

the ownership of undertakings, in particular in the event of mergers.

(6) The designation as an immediate objective of the overall application of the principle of the standard 40-hour working week by 1975, and the principle of four weeks' annual paid holiday by 1976.

(7) The setting up of a European foundation for the improvement of the environment and of living and working conditions.

Other measures in the programme, significant but not designated as priorities, included the following:

(1) A long-term programme for the social re-integration of handicapped people.

(2) The extension of social protection, including possibly the "dynamisation" of social security benefits.

(3) The establishment of a European Trade Union Institute.

(4) Measures to help unemployed school-leavers.

(5) The development of the European social budget (see Chapter 6).

(6) Examination of measures to improve minimum wages throughout the Community and of the scope for Community action on asset formation.

(7) Health protection against pollution and environmental hazards and extension of the programme for radiation protection.

(8) Extension of the E.C.S.C. housing programme to assist other special categories in need, particularly the handicapped and migrants.

These proposals, together with a number of measures to improve Community statistics on social indicators, industrial accidents and safety, incomes and assets, and labour market forecasts, made up the core of the action programme. The reader who feels somewhat bewildered by this catalogue may be reassured; subsequent chapters will explain the thinking behind the various proposals and what happened to them in the ensuing three years. The reader who feels he is being presented with a somewhat indiscriminate "laundry list" of actions, no doubt good and important in themselves, but not linked by any clearly visible principle emanating from the Treaty of Rome, may take heart; his impression is broadly correct. The programme was prepared very quickly to meet the imperative demands of the end-1972 summit. It consisted of measures for which it was felt, rightly or wrongly, that there was a broad political consensus among the nine member-governments, and which collectively might go quite a long way to meet the political and social needs described in the previous chapter. The priorities in the programme thus reflected a political judgement of what was thought to be both desirable and possible, rather than a juridical judgement of what were thought to be the social policy implications of the Rome Treaty.

And indeed it could hardly be otherwise. A social policy based on the priorities of the Treaty would be bound to focus around two principles — the free movement of labour and the equalisation of competitive conditions between enterprises. The social action programme certainly contained elements of the former principle in its proposals for making the European labour market more "transparent" (consultation on employment policies and improvement of labour market forecasts), and in the migrants' action programme in so far as this related to migrant workers from Community countries (primarily Italians and Irish). But a social action programme limited to this principle would hardly be seen as responding to the political and social needs of the mid-1970s.

A social action programme based on the principle of equalising competitive costs might, by contrast, be a very far-reaching programme indeed. For social costs fall directly or indirectly on enterprises, and one might well therefore argue that logically a Common Market requires the harmonisation of social systems throughout the Community, just as it requires harmonised energy and transport policies, harmonised tax systems and interest rates (none of which, incidentally, it has got at the time of writing in late 1976).

It is true that the Commission has justified a number of proposals which have important social implications — the draft directives on labour law in the social action programme (on collective dismissals and the preservation of workers' rights after a merger), and those on company law reform (including the famous Fifth Directive on worker participation and the subsequent so-called "Green Paper") — at least partly on the need to equalise competitive conditions. But in the labour law directives it has gone out of its way to stress that it is seeking only to establish minimum provisions on which national governments and individual enterprises should seek to improve wherever possible; and neither in the labour law directives nor those on company law does it imply that harmonisation for its own sake, regardless of content, is a major objective. In Community jargon, the goal is "harmonisation in progress" or upward harmonisation.

We shall have to examine in Chapter 6 the scope for a more ambitious harmonisation of the various social systems of the Nine. Suffice to say here that the view taken by the Commission in 1974 — I am sure rightly — was that the scope for such harmonisation in the immediate future was extremely limited, given the diversity in standards, systems, priorities and values among the member-States; and that what the Community institutions should rather be seeking to do was to establish if there were any categories of people who, for one reason or another, were falling below what might be regarded as an acceptable norm for such a wealthy and advanced group of countries as the members of the European Community, and concentrate first on helping them; and then seek gradually to level up towards what might be regarded as an acceptable Community average. The other point that needs to be made is that the equalisation of costs, while it may have sound scriptural justification in the Rome Treaty, is hardly a ringing clarion call to social reform. There must be more cogent reasons for seeking to do good!

So we come back to the problem posed in the previous chapter. The measures proposed by the Commission in its social action programme did not, because they could not, flow logically from the Rome Treaty. This is not to say that any of them were contrary to or out of line with the broad principles of the Treaty. But the Treaty does not actually *require* a social programme of this kind. Its justification is political, not juridical. The question thus has to be posed: Is there a need for a Community social programme at all as opposed to national social policies? We shall have to come back to this question at the end of this book. It was a question which it was not fashionable to ask in the climate of 1973 - 74. But as economic conditions worsened during 1974 and after, one noticed in Brussels a growing tendency to query the desirability, not of this particular social action programme but of *any* Community social programme which did not flow inescapably from the Rome Treaty provisions.

As the political and economic storm-clouds darkened, however, the Commission proceeded doggedly to work through the social programme, submitting proposals under all the main heads requested by the Council. And in fact the success rate during 1974 and 1975 was quite high, especially by comparison with some other areas of Community activity. Thus in 1974 the Council of Ministers approved the opening of the Social Fund for migrants and handicapped workers; the establishment of the European Vocational Training Centre, the Foundation for Improved Living and Working Conditions, and the General Safety Committee (with expanded terms of reference for the Mines Safety Committee); directives on equal pay and on mass dismissals; and the action programme on the rehabilitation of handicapped workers. In 1975 the Council adopted the poverty programme, the principle of the 40-hour week and 4 weeks' annual paid holidays, a draft resolution setting out the principles of the migrants action programme, and a directive establishing equality of opportunity for women in the labour market. It also approved two extensions of the Social Fund not specified in the social action programme, to help workers aged under 25 and workers in the clothing industry. A number of other measures in the action programme were implemented without requiring specific ministerial approval; for example, the establishment of consultation between the member-States (under the aegis of the Commission) on employment and social protection policies; the extension of the social budget; and detailed proposals relating to the action programme on health and safety and to the humanisation of work (what the social action programme rather obscurely calls "the organisation of tasks").

By the end of 1975 the social action programme as a whole was running up to schedule, and it looked as if the whole programme would be completed on time by the end of 1976. The measures on environmental and radiation protection, a series of directives on pollution from air, water or noxious substances, were also making progress, if slowly, through the Council of Ministers. Moreover, the resources available for the Social Fund were showing a rather spectacular expansion — from around £30 million in 1971 to more than £250 million by the end of 1975. This indicated not only the increased willingness of member-States to pay money into the Community for social purposes but also the increasing concern with unemployment as a major social and economic problem in the Community from mid-1974 onwards.

Unemployment also gave a spur to the "participation" element in the social action programme. At the end of 1974 the trade unions agreed to end their boycott of the so-called Standing Committee on Employment, a tripartite body operating at European level embracing leaders of employer organisations and trade unions, ministers of labour or social affairs of the Nine, and the Commission. This body, established in 1971 to examine all issues connected with employment at Community level, had been defunct for some time because of difficulties as to membership within the trade unions. However, under the stresses of the recession in 1974 the unions agreed to a formula which enabled the Committee to be reactivated — and indeed during 1975 and 1976 on occasion to be enlarged to include the ministers of finance or economics, whose policies in fact have far more influence on the level of employment in member-States than anything which labour or employment ministers can do. Thus a major step forward was taken during 1975 to establish a tripartite dialogue on the evolution of Community economic and social policy in so far as it affects jobs.

However, while progress was being made on social policy during 1974 and 1975, there was a growing tendency to emasculate policies which like the poverty programme involved the expenditure of Community money, or which like the 40-hour week and 4 weeks' holiday could be costly to industry (where the date of introduction was postponed to end-1978). The reluctance of the richer countries to underwrite Community schemes which would benefit the poorer was especially marked in the case of the Regional Fund, which was only finally approved, on a much more modest scale than originally envisaged, in 1975. In fact the Regional Fund has emerged as about the same size as the Social Fund, which grew by degrees, while the original grandiose plans for the Regional Fund were blocked. (The relationship, present and future, between the two Funds is analysed in Chapter 3.)

The debacle of the social action programme came in its third year. Progress on the remaining parts of the programme — including, most importantly, the substance of the migrants programme ((discussed in detail in Chapter 4), and the various measures concerned with incomes and social protection (Chapter 7) — slowed to a trickle, and it was already clear before the end of the year that the programme could not be completed on schedule. This may not have been altogether unwelcome to some members of the outgoing Commission or to certain member-State governments, despite their unanimous endorsement of the original programme.

For the Community as a whole was moving backwards during 1974 - 76.

There is a melancholy irony about the 1972 summit statement that "the heads of government would attach as much importance to vigorous action in the social field as to achievement of economic and monetary union". If progress in the social field at Community level was disappointing, progress in the E.M.U. was totally negative. Despite expectations and promises, the British and Irish pounds and the Italian lira remained outside the E.M.U. thoughout the entire three-year period. In 1975 they were joined by the French franc as France's economy began to lose its competitive edge. The E.M.U. had become essentially a "Deutschmark area". The economic crisis led to a steady polarisation of the Nine into strong and weak economies, reflecting more than anything else the different will or ability of governments to control their domestic inflations. During 1974 - 76 the inflation rate in the United Kingdom, Italy and Ireland was more than three times that in West Germany. The rate in France, Benelux and Denmark averated nearly twice that in Germany. In a Common Market, with minimal restrictions on intra-Community trade, the effect of such differences in the inflation rate was inevitably quickly felt on the balance of payments and thus on the exchange rate of currencies. So the currencies of the weak countries continued to depreciate against those of the strong. West Germany moved into a massive surplus position on its balance of payments *vis-à-vis* the rest of the Community, despite exchange rate changes. The three weak members of the Community incurred equally massive payments deficits.

The widening gap between the strong and the weak members of the Community put increasing strains on Community solidarity, on the willingness and ability of the different member-States to work together. In the social policy field the divergence of objectives became more and more marked. For the poorer members the social policy priority was above all the use of Community resources to create more jobs in the weaker regions through massive increases in the Regional and Social Fund. Other aspects of the social action programme — especially those, like the directives on labour law, which might add to industrial costs — were of considerably less interest at a time of economic stringency.

For the richer members, however, the prospect of a transfer of resources via the Brussels bureaucracy for the benefit of countries who were manifestly not running their economies very well, was unwelcome. For them, social policy needed to concern itself with the raising of standards throughout the Community — provided that the costs did not fall exclusively on the richer members. So thinking about social policy at the European level has had to come to grips with the delicate issue of the willingness of the Community to contemplate a systematic transfer of resources between member-States to help the poorer members to level up their standards towards those of the rich. We shall have to return to this question in Chapter 9 in the context of the future Community budget.

Despite the divergence of economies reflecting differing rates of success in controlling inflation, there was one common factor facing all the Nine from 1974 onwards — unacceptably high rates of unemployment. When the social action programme was launched at the beginning of 1974 the problems in the labour market were marginal. Broadly speaking, the Community enjoyed full employment, but there were regions and groups which were exceptions to the general rule. Within 12 months the perspective had changed completely. Unemployment among the Community's 100 million work-force had jumped from around 2½% to well over 5%. Unemployment and inflation had become the two issues which above all pre-occupied the man and woman in the street. If the European Community could not solve these issues it would have difficulty retaining the loyalty of its citizens, and it would not be well placed to resist demands for sectional protectionism which could only too easily snowball to a point at which the Common Market itself would be in danger. This was the very real danger confronting the Community institutions at the end of 1976.

In looking at the various aspects of social policy in this overall context it is as well to start therefore with the central issue of employment. To this we shall now turn.

CHAPTER 3

Employment and the European Social Fund

After its frightening rise during 1974 and 1975, the rate of unemployment in the European Community levelled off in 1976. But at the year-end it was still unacceptably high, and all the evidence suggested that it would remain so up to 1980 and beyond. The rate of economic recovery predicted for the Nine would not be such as to restore the employment rate to what it was before the 1974 recession. This is a basic datum for the next stage of European social policy. The various discussions which have been held in the Standing Committee on Employment, in the broader meetings attended also by finance ministers, in the regular discussions between director-generals of employment ministries convened by the Commission, in the meetings of the forecasting experts, have all served to underline this dismal prediction. But to the dismay of the "social partners" — the representatives of employers and trade unions — they have not been able to come up with any dramatic solution. The problem is essentially economic, not social. But if the economic problems remain insoluble, there will be mounting pressure for social solutions.

What does this mean? It means, first, that Europe has to consider the full implications of a commitment to full employment. Hitherto it has been assumed that the full employment to which each of the member-States is formally committed will flow automatically from the correct pursuit of macro-economic policies — supplemented in the case of Ireland and Italy by freedom to emigrate to more prosperous member-countries. In other words, governments only had to get the balance of supply and demand right and full employment would follow. But now, for the first time since 1945, it begins to look as though the long-term natural growth rate of the Community's economies may be too low to provide jobs for all who seek them — unless special measures are taken to create job vacancies over and above those that would flow anyway from macro-economic policies.

Such measures could take a number of forms. One would be to lower the retirement age throughout the Community or to move towards a radically shorter working week (without compensatory overtime). Another would be to concentrate on labour-intensive rather than capital-intensive investments through some form of fiscal or other incentive. A third would be to develop what is coming to be called the ''secondary labour market'' — the provision of jobs by public authorities outside the market economy to carry out community projects of one kind or another.

Some member-States have taken tentative steps in these directions, but a full-scale Community action on any one of these fronts would pose a number of difficulties. The most obvious is the damaging impact on labour costs at a time when the Community countries are perforce trying to boost exports to meet increased oil bills and to retain job opportunities in exporting industries. There is the high cost in terms of public expenditure of community employment projects — let alone the resistance of trade unions to enforced early retirement for their members, or to undercutting of wage rates by the employment of cheap labour in the secondary job market. So any programme of planned work-sharing or work-spreading needs to be looked at very carefully before commitment.

At the same time such measures cannot be excluded. One of the most alarming features of the recession has been the way in which in every Community country the main burden of redundancy has fallen on the young — the under-25s, even more so the under-21s. The dangers to society of the existence of a hard core of (often highly qualified) structurally unemployed young people need no underlining. The reasons for the phenomenon are not far to seek. Most employers practise — with the approval of trade unions — ''last-in-first-out'' redundancy policies. So when jobs shrink it is those with least seniority — in other words the young — who are normally the first to go. Second, many more girls than in the past are competing for jobs; to some extent, therefore, the youthful labour market is becoming overcrowded due to competition between the sexes. Third, and more fundamental, young labour is no longer cheap labour. The former differentials between mature and young workers have been progressively eroded away by governmental and union action; so the former incentives for employers to give preference to young workers no longer apply.

All these factors are explicable. But there is a further element in the situation, apparently very widespread in the European Community, which is unacceptable and which should yield to treatment. This is the existence of a major mismatch — a failure of communication, a conflict of objectives — between the world of education and training and the world of jobs.

Briefly, far too many youngsters are emerging from the education system with an attitude to the business world, in which the majority hope to earn their living and build their career, compounded of hostility, exaggerated expectation and a high degree of ignorance. They have been ill-prepared for the reality of the business world. As a result, for many of them the first period at work is one of frequent moves in order to find a job more in accord with their expectations — a process which gives them a reputation with employers for unreliability and restlessness.

One way of tackling the problem of youthful unemployment therefore is to put more effort and more resources into the provision of vocational *guidance* as opposed to vocational *training*. This is essentially a matter for member-States rather than for the Community institutions.

A second category of people hard hit by the recession are *women*. It will be recalled that one of the main priorities of the social action programme was to improve the position of women in the labour market. Article 119 of the Rome Treaty was supposed to guarantee women equal pay for equal work, but in fact it proved a weak provision when tested in the Courts, and in 1974 the Council of Ministers accepted a Commission directive which gave women much greater protection. This was followed the next year by a directive designed to make illegal discrimination against women at the place of work — in recruitment to jobs, promotion and access to training. The directive was accompanied by a memorandum — on which the Council took no action — listing a number of practical problems outside the legal field which faced women at work: problems of education, of vocational training, above all of reconciling family responsibilities with employment requirements. The memorandum provides a basis for a series of measures over the next few years to improve the prospects of women at work.

Unfortunately, the demand for more work opportunities by women has come at precisely the time when job opportunities as a whole are shrinking. So this demand, which can hardly be resisted, is a further complication in the overall employment situation facing Europe.

Not much needs to be said about the third main "underprivileged

group" — the handicapped. As already indicated, the handicapped enjoy a special priority position within the Social Fund, and the Community operates — albeit on a modest scale — an action programme in favour of rehabilitation schemes for the disabled: a programme which consists largely of the exchange of techniques and personnel between designated "centres of excellence" among rehabilitation centres, and the promotion of research into schemes for rehabilitation. The Community has recognised a special responsibility for the disabled. But clearly, when overall employment prospects are bad, those for the disabled worsen proportionally. (The long-term programme for the social reintegration of handicapped people, on which the Commission was supposed to present proposals by end-1976, differs from the action programme in that it is supposed to concern itself with those whose handicap is such that they can never be re-integrated into normal working life.)

In the original social action programme, older workers were classified as a potential problem group along with the young, women and the handicapped. But in the discussions since 1974 there has been no support for special actions to help older workers — an indication, perhaps, that they have been less badly hit by the recession than the young. It is also significant, perhaps, that despite all the lip-service paid by member-States to the need for a better deal for women at work, there has been no support at all for suggestions made by the Commission that the Social Fund should be used to help finance special training schemes for women; for example, to meet the re-training problems of women returning to work after many years' absence bringing up a family.

Bearing in mind the general question posed at the end of Chapter 1 — Does the Community have a role to play in European social policy, and if so, what? — perhaps one should pose the issue specifically as regards employment. The Community has traditionally assumed that it has a role in helping the under-dog in the labour market — the worker in a high-unemployment region, the disabled, and so on. Clearly the problems of these groups become no less urgent when the overall employment market turns down; indeed, the reverse is true. At the same time, if one concentrates one's attention completely on the so-called marginal groups, it may simply be at the expense of the adult males who are not normally in need of help. There is no particular sense in that. Neither socially, economically nor politically is there much merit in boosting employment of youths, women or handicapped if it means proportionally fewer jobs for fully trained fathers of families. So what is the scope for Community action on general employment levels?

Obviously the Community institutions have a role to play in assisting co-ordination of national policies on employment, employment forecasts and, indeed, economic policy in general. This is being done. At prime-ministerial level there are now regular meetings at least three times a year .to co-ordinate overall economic strategy in the Community. As already mentioned, there are frequent meetings, under the auspices of the Council of Ministers or the Commission, of those concerned with employment policy at national level. The importance of this catalytic function of the Commission should not be underestimated — we shall see it at work in other fields of social policy too in later chapters — but clearly it cannot by itself be a substitute for policy failures at national level. Brussels has no magic wand for problem-solving denied to national governments.

Brussels does, however, have an interest in seeing that in their attempts to solve national problems member-States do not promote autarkic solutions at the Community's expense; for example, by subsidising jobs in particular uneconomic industries at the expense of competitors in other Community countries, or by erecting barriers to free trade within the Common Market. There must be no return to the "beggar-my-neighbour" nationalist policies of the 1930s. This means that wherever possible Community solutions must be sought.

One way in which this can be done is by promoting labour *mobility* in a vocational rather than a geographical sense. (We shall be discussing geographical mobility in the next chapter.) The traditional means by which this has been tackled at Community level has been by actions to promote and encourage vocational training. This interest has been given an important fillip by the establishment in 1975 of a European Centre for the Development of Vocational Training, located in West Berlin with a tripartite governing council consisting of representatives of national governments, the social partners and the Commission. (I had the honour to be its first president.)

The major weapon at the Community's disposal for boosting labour mobility is, of course, the *Social Fund*. During the 1960s the Social Fund played, as already indicated, a fairly minor role in assisting in the retraining and resettlement of workers from declining sectors. During the whole decade some $421 million were spent on Community-approved schemes involving some 1.43 million workers. The budget, however, was limited and the Commission had no possibility of initiating schemes, but could only react to proposals put forward by member-governments. So far from being a mechanism for transferring resources from richer to poorer countries, the Social Fund conferred more funds on West Germany than on any other country.

In 1971 the Fund was fundamentally changed. The new Fund started to operate in 1972. It was divided into two Articles with separate budgets. Under Article 4 money can be given, on a fifty-fifty basis with public national authorities, to help workers whose jobs may be threatened as a direct result of continuing integration in the Community. Areas for such intervention have to be specifically designated by the Council of Ministers. At the present time (1976) such areas are: workers moving out of agriculture, textile and clothing workers, migrants, handicapped workers (especially those in schemes covered by the Community's handicapped action programme), and workers aged under 25.

Second, under article 5 the Social Fund can advance money — under the same fifty-fifty conditions — for the correction of unsatisfactory employment situations, especially in backward or declining regions and in industries affected by technical progress. Handicapped workers can also benefit under Article 5. It will be seen that the rules for Article 5 are much looser than for Article 4, and until Article 4 was opened to schemes for young workers in 1975 the Fund was in the embarrassing position of having surplus, non-transferable, money under Article 4 and a huge surplus of claims over funds available under Article 5. Rather over 60% of the money in Article 5 normally goes to projects in regions in difficulty, which means that the lion's share goes to the United Kingdom, Italy and (on a *per capita* basis) Ireland. These countries therefore constitute a permanent lobby for the increase of resources under Article 5. By contrast, spending under Article 4 is more evenly distributed between member-States, but overall the main beneficiaries of the Fund are the poorer countries while most of the budget is funded by the richer. In these circumstances it is perhaps quite an achievement that over the period 1972 - 6 the Social Fund's budget expanded by nearly 500% to around $500 million.

Nevertheless, nobody is very happy about the Social Fund. When it was established in its new form provision was made for a fundamental review after 5 years, and the Commission has to bring forward proposals for reform before the end of 1977. The debate in fact started in 1976, and it is already clear what some of the protagonists will be arguing. Some of the member-States will ask that the Commission should lose much of the present discretion it has under the Fund rules to promote some schemes submitted by member-States and reject others. (In this it is assisted by an advisory committee on which sit representatives of the social partners as well as national governments.) This could be done, very simply, by establishing national quotas for Fund aid, so that each member-State was formally entitled to an agreed share of the budget to be spent more or less how it chose. This would reduce the bureaucracy in Brussels concerned with administering the Fund but would destroy any pretensions which the Fund might have to concern with the *quality* of training and retraining schemes.

This links closely with another issue where the Commission is at odds with some of the member-States. The Commission argues that aid under the Social Fund should not simply underwrite national schemes which would otherwise be financed out of national budgets but should provide *additional* aid; that is, it should help to finance activities which would not otherwise be carried on — especially activities which, because of their pioneering character or some other special attribute, might provide guidance or inspiration for other countries. Clearly this would be impossible if the Fund moved to a national quota basis.

The corollary is that the growth of the Social Fund would almost certainly be less than it would if the "additionality principle" were generally accepted. This is because the West German Government, to take just one example, is less ready to subsidise the British, Irish or Italian taxpayer than it is to support Community initiatives. On the other hand, it would be perverse if the Social Fund managers were to give priority in every case to schemes which the national authorities — who are after all the main experts — judged to be marginal. The answer, in my view, is for the Fund's operations to be planned in conjunction with long-term plans submitted by the different national authorities, so that the vocational training aid which the Fund can provide is related, on the one hand, to national manpower plans, and, on the other, to particular Community priorities which should be discussed by the Standing Committee on Employment or some specially designated section thereof.

A second issue which undoubtedly has to be discussed is whether the Fund can be used more effectively as a device to promote short-term employment or to ease the fluctuations of the business cycle on the job market. Attempts to use the Fund to deal with the main casualties of the 1974 - 6 recession were not very successful. On more than one occasion the Commission tried to get governments to agree on a short list of threatened industries to which priority aid could be given for retraining and redeployment. But it was never possible to get the nine countries to agree on a list of industries since the industrial structure and priorities differ in each member-State.

Nor have the Fund managers had any success to date in getting agreement to a list of *growth* industries or activities for which workers benefiting from Fund aid should be trained. This pinpoints one of the inevitable defects of an institution like the Social Fund as a counter-cyclical operator. The Fund is concerned with the redeployment of workers from declining to expanding, or at least potentially expanding, sectors. In a general recession it is not hard to identify industries in the former category but much harder to identify those in the latter.

My own view is that the attempt to install national quotas for Social Fund aid should be resisted and that its rules should be made more flexible to enable the money to be used more effectively. I believe that the distinction between Article 4 and Article 5 has become a needless bureaucratic obstacle which should be abolished. Its irrelevance is shown by the fact that aid for the handicapped can be given under either Article. Second, I would like to see a relaxation of the rule under which Social Fund aid has to be exactly matched by a national contribution — neither more nor less than 50%. This, too, imports an unnecessary rigidity into the Fund's operations. In some cases projects do not need as big an injection of Community money as 50% to get them off the ground. In other cases, where the Commission feels there is a particular Community interest in a particular project, it ought to be allowed to advance much more than 50% of the cost — so that it would itself be, in effect, the major partner in particular schemes. Ideally, I would like to see the Commission have the power to vary its assistance to projects from, say, 90% down to, say, 10%. But it would have to be publicly accountable for its decision in each case, as it is now.

However, it is not really meaningful to consider the Social Fund in isolation. After all, it accounts for not more than around 6% of the estimated total public expenditure on training and retraining in the nine member-States. Its role, therefore, is bound to be marginal overall. In order to make a useful impact, therefore, its operations have to be linked to some kind of national strategies in each member-State — strategies based on reasonably accurate manpower forecasts. The problem is that manpower plans in this sense hardly exist in many of the Nine.

Equally important is that the Commission should exercise a better co-ordination of its own instruments. In addition to the Social Fund there is now the *Regional Fund*, disposing of approximately equal resources. There is the guidance section of the common agricultural policy (F.E.O.G.A) which helps to finance farmers leaving the land; and there is the European Investment Bank which provides cheap loans for employment-creating projects. Surely it is not unfair to ask that the Commission uses these instruments in a reasonably co-ordinated way?

The relationship between the Regional and Social Funds is especially important in this context. More than half the total budget of the Social Fund is spent in the regions covered by the Regional Fund. In many ways the two Funds are complementary. The Regional Fund is designed to stimulate *demand* for jobs by subsidising investment in the regions. The Social Fund operates on the *supply* side by ensuring a supply of adequately trained workers in the appropriate locality. So the two Funds should cerrainly operate in an integrated way.

It is also the case that a single, integrated Fund could make much more of a strategic impact than two separate Funds with limited resources, and the Commission would appear more credible as a Fund manager if it was not frittering away its limited management resources on separate but overlapping activities. On the other hand, a merger between the two Funds would present certain problems. The Regional Fund has moved much nearer to a national quota system than the Social Fund. There is no equivalent of the Social Fund Advisory Committee, on which the social partners are represented, to advise the managers of the Regional Fund. The consultative body is entirely governmental. And, while the Fund still has the discretion to reject national claims — and the arguments over "additionality" are exactly the same in the case of the Regional as of the Social Fund — there is an agreement between the member-governments as to the right allocation of resources from the Regional Fund which is nearly, if not quite, the same thing as a national quota system. The United Kingdom has, in other words, an entitlement to a certain share of the Fund, and if it only forwards claims up to the level of its entitlement it is hard for the Regional Fund managers to reject them. Thus the kind of debate between claims which takes place in the Social Fund Advisory Committee, which must lead to an improvement in the quality of the claims, cannot really take place within the Regional Fund structure unless governments gratuitously present the Fund with more claims than they are entitled to, thus leaving the question of choice between claimants to the Fund — which of course may have certain domestic political advantages.

Thus, if there is to be (as I would hope) an eventual merger of the two Funds — into what might be called a Community Employment Fund — there will have to be some changes in the structure and constitution of both Funds; and it would be vital, in my view, that the combined Fund should provide a continuing freedom to choose between claims without the constraints of national quotas. It should be, in other words, an instrument for a *Community* employment policy rather than a rather clumsy means of transferring money from one country to another.

Until the Community has a clear idea how to use the instruments already at its disposal, it seems to me premature to envisage new instruments. What has to be done is:

(a) to set overall employment targets for each country and for the Community as a whole in the context of a viable macro-economic strategy;

(b) to relate the expected demand under broad categories to the anticipated supply of workers, based on demographic and educational trends;

(c) to identify particular areas of anticipated mismatch between demand and supply;

(d) to use the existing Community instruments, suitably reformed, to remedy these mismatches.

This is easy to say but of course vastly more difficult to do. One major complication is the fact that the Community is not a collection of nine discrete labour markets but a single labour market practising free movement of labour — albeit with certain imperfections. Thus, in trying to develop an overall employment policy using best forecasting techniques it is necessary to look carefully at movements of labour both within the Community and between the Community and third countries. It is to this crucial area of employment policy and, indeed, of social policy as a whole that we turn in the next chapter.

CHAPTER 4

Migration and Regional Development

The freedom of workers to move throughout the Community in search of jobs is one of the basic principles of the Treaty of Rome. In principle there is a single Community-wide labour market to which all E.E.C. citizens have equal access. In fact of course this labour market is shot through with imperfections. So far as professional workers are concerned there are as yet few diplomas or qualifications recognised as being of equal status in all the Community countries. This necessarily restricts the ability of professionals in all but a few cases to practise in other E.E.C. countries.

At the level of the industrial worker the two main problems are the lack of knowledge of job opportunities in other countries and the numerous social and bureaucratic problems connected with living and working in an alien community. As regards the former, the Commission has been striving for many years to establish a computerised information system on job vacancies to which the nine national employment agencies would subscribe, using an agreed job classification notation, so that a vacancy, say, for a skilled welder in Bremen would be transmitted immediately to labour exchanges in, say, Palermo or Newcastle, which were known through the system to have people with the right skills on their books. This system, code-named SEDOC, to be operated by a European Coordination Office for Employment — code-named BECODE, a kind of all-European labour exchange — is at the time of writing in 1976 in its final running-in stage.

If the system can be made to work effectively — and the technical problems are formidable — it will remove a long-standing irritant in relations between two Community countries, West Germany and Italy, in particular. Italy is the biggest labour exporter within the E.E.C., Germany the biggest labour importer. For many years the Italians have been complaining that they have not been getting adequate information from the German authorities about job vacancies in Germany, with the result that jobs which could be filled by Italians go instead to Turks, Yugoslavs or Greeks. The Germans for their part have regularly laid the blame on the alleged inadequacies of the Italian placement system in processing inquiries without inordinate delay. My own view is that there has been some right on both sides. The Commission has tried to act as a go-between by encouraging a regular exchange of personnel between the placement agencies of the two countries — a bilateral exchange which is now being extended also to the Benelux countries. For the time being the issue may be academic in view of the limited job opportunities of any kind in the E.E.C. and the restriction on import of workers from outside the Community. Nevertheless, it is clearly important for the smooth functioning of the Community's economy, as well as for the well-being of its citizens, that the labour market should be as fully "transparent" as possible, with the maximum amount of information regarding not only present demand and supply in different locations and categories, but also expectations for the future on which training and other relevant programmes can be based.

The other obstacle to free movement within the Community — discrimination of one kind or another practised against the foreign worker — was the subject of a special Regulation (No. 1612) passed in 1968. This Regulation stipulated that the foreign worker was entitled to full equality with the domestic worker in all matters pertaining to employment, remuneration and working conditions, including basic social security. The problems of implementing this regulation have proved considerable.

Migration within the E.E.C. was largely a domestic issue until the 1960s. In 1959 about three-quarters of the migrant workers in the then Community of Six came from within the E.E.C. — overwhelmingly from Italy. But the great boom of the 1960s stimulated one of the major waves of immigration in modern history, and it came largely from outside the Community. By 1973 the number of migrants living and working in the enlarged Community of Nine was estimated to be between 10 and 12 million — in other words, greater than the population of Belgium and a little less than that of the Netherlands. Moreover, of this total (which includes dependants as well as actual workers) more than two-thirds came from non-E.E.C. countries: Turks, Greeks, Yugoslavs, Spaniards, Portuguese, North Africans, West Indians and people from the Indian sub-continent making up the largest contingents from the third world, with Italians and

Irish constituting the largest groups of Community migrants. Migrants accounted for some 5 % of the total E.E.C. labour force.

This mass influx of peoples had important effects on the economies and societies of the Community. First, of course, it removed what might otherwise have been a brake on expansion. It gave the system a very much greater degree of flexibility than it might otherwise have had. The migrants were ready to do the jobs which Community citizens increasingly shunned — the low-paid "dirty" jobs in the public sector, and the boring repetitive jobs in assembly-line industries such as motor-car manufacture. For this reason employers in E.E.C. industry had less incentive than, say, the Swedes to invest heavily in making jobs more attractive. Moreover, since many of the third-country migrants entered the Community on short-term contracts — typically for one or two years — they provided a balancing factor. When market conditions changed, or industry was undergoing structural alterations, it was the migrants on short-term contracts who were dispensable. Or so the theory went.

As against these advantages, there were two major drawbacks from the Community's point of view. One was that the very ease of migration encouraged the centripetal tendencies of the E.E.C., with the result that the outer regions failed to attract the capital investment they might have expected when the central regions ran out of native labour, and instead of importing capital found themselves losing their best-qualified people who were forced to join the great migration. To some extent the encouragement of migration — taking the worker to the job — runs counter to the principles of regional development, and also to the long-term principles of overseas aid; in other words, rather than import Turkish or Portuguese workers the E.E.C. countries should be putting down new plant in those countries so that the workers there do not have to leave their families and homes.

It is quite true that in the long term the best interests of both the E.E.C. and the Mediterranean "fringe" would be served by a planned programme of taking jobs to the worker. It is also true, as the Community has recognised, that measures to help migration within the E.E.C. should be balanced by a vigorous programme of regional development. But both these are going to take a long time, and in the meantime there are two stubborn facts which cannot be wished away. One is that the Treaty of Rome confers the right of free movement and equality of treatment in jobs on all E.E.C. citizens. The second is that, whether it likes it or not, the Community has acquired an alien population of upwards of 10 million people who have somehow to be absorbed and catered for.

One further point of principle has to be discussed before we can turn to the detailed issues of migration. To what extent can or should the Community discriminate between Community migrants and those from third countries? I think the distinction that has to be drawn is between the right to seek work and rights once accepted in work. On the first count, it is quite reasonable that the migrant from within the Community should have preferential treatment to the third country migrant. After all, we have already seen that the Treaty of Rome guarantees equal access to jobs to all Community citizens. If the Community is to retain any control over its labour market, this must imply a discrimination against third-country immigrants.

In fact, during the boom years before 1974 there may have been a *de facto* advantage in job-seeking for third-country citizens. The bilateral arrangements, for example, between the German labour-hiring public agency, the *Bundesanstalt für Arbeit,* and its Turkish opposite number, worked a good deal more smoothly than the more decentralised system in force between the German and Italian employment agencies. And the Turks had the added advantage of security of tenure for the duration of their service contract.

So it is entirely reasonable that Italians should have priority in access to jobs over, say, Turks or Yugoslavs. And there are some other areas — for example, political rights —where it is not unreasonable to apply double standards between migrants from Community countries and others. But there is no justification for such discrimination when it comes to *social* rights and benefits. Once the Community accepts a migrant from anywhere in the world as a worker it must be prepared to give him or her the elementary rights of citizenship in the social sphere.

Up to now the Community's acceptance of this principle has been patchy. And here we come to the second major drawback which the huge immigration of the 1960s has had for the countries of the Community. For obvious reasons, the migrants have tended to concentrate in "ghetto" areas of the big cities, and their presence has put heavy strains on the social infrastructure and caused certain environmental problems.

This has not been the fault of the immigrants themselves. The blame must be laid at the door of a system which has sought to use their labour without taking adequate account of their needs as people, of the problems of integration and assimilation between them and their indigenous neighbours. The problems are most intense when the immigrants are of a different colour from the indigenous people — as with Indians and Caribbeans in the United Kingdom, Algerians in France, more recently Surinamese in the Netherlands. But the problems are there, in greater or lesser degree, wherever there are concentrations of peoples with a recognisably different cultural and linguistic background to their hosts. And throughout the E.E.C., during the 1960s and early 1970s, one could see a developing situation with frightening parallels to the United States — the growing concentration, mainly in the decaying centres of big cities, of an embittered and depressed sub-proletariat of immigrant peoples, excluded from the more prosperous society around them, tolerated as workers but not accepted as citizens.

The main discriminations suffered by migrant communities in living and working conditions have been in the areas of access to vocational training, education for their children, housing, health services and social security (as regards third-country migrants; for Community migrants this is covered by Regulation 1612/68).

It is to these matters that the action programme on migrants prepared by the Commission as part of its social action programme mainly addresses itself. As regards vocational training, the opening of Article 4 of the Social Fund to schemes for migrants has a dual purpose. For Community migrants the Fund can now provide comprehensive assistance, helping to finance the movement of the worker and his family from his home to the place of work and back again when his work contract expires, as well as the training needed to enable him to perform the work. For third-country migrants the Fund can only be used for training and not for transportation.

It is no accident that the first part of the migrants' programme to be implemented should have concerned itself with training. One of the myths which encouraged the mass migration of the 1960s was that the industrialised countries of the E.E.C. would help the development of the Mediterranean economies by giving their citizens ''on-the-job'' training in industrial skills which the migrants could then apply in their own countries on their return home. But, by and large, this has not happened. The migrants, especially those from third countries, have tended to find themselves restricted to low-paid, unskilled work, shut out from opportunities of advancement. This is a discrimination which is ultimately indefensible, and which the opening of the Social Fund is designed to end.

But some of the training which the migrant worker needs is more elementary than that. In many cases migrant workers need basic training in the language of the host country to enable them to perform even simple tasks — and also to ensure that they can understand basic safety instructions enough not to be a hazard to themselves and their work-mates. Some of the bilateral agreements — for example, that between Germany and Turkey — provide for basic language training before the migrant leaves his home country. But experience shows that this has not been very effective.

There is a clear need for adequate reception facilities for migrants and their families to ensure that they have access to the basic health and welfare services of their host countries. These exist in some towns and countries but by no means in all. And, since migrants are increasingly bringing their families with them, there is an evident need to ensure that their children receive education both in the language and culture of their mother country and in that of the host country. A directive to that effect is one of the first measures proposed in the Community's migrant programme.

The issue of social security for third-country migrants is more complex. The situation varies from country to country as a result of a series of bilateral agreements over the years. The long-term objective must be to remove the various discriminations at present in existence and bring the situation for third-country migrants in line with that for Community migrants. At the same time, there are important problems still to be resolved for some classes of Community migrants also as regards the payment of family benefits. Some host countries pay the migrant the benefits in force in his country of origin, some those in force in the country of employment. Plainly there is a need for standardisation so long as the level of benefits varies from one Community country to another (as will be the case for a considerable time to come). The question of exporting family benefits is also a complex one, especially for third-country migrants. How is one to check effectively on the family circumstances of an immigrant from a village in Bangladesh or Nigeria? How does one adjust provisions tailored to the "nuclear family" tradition of Western European society to the very different cultures of Islam? The practical problems are fearsome. But that is no excuse for denying to the migrant the basic welfare state provisions in force in the society within which he is working and to which he is obliged to pay taxes.

The need, therefore, is to try to ensure that over a period of years the living and working conditions of third-country migrants approximate to those of Community migrants by liberalising and rationalising the system of bilaterally negotiated work permits, so that it increasingly approximates to the conditions applying to Community migrants under Regulation 1612/68. The present jungle of social security regulations needs to be rationalised both for Community and third-country migrants, so that there is a uniform system for payment of family benefits, the co-ordination through Community legislation of non-contributory schemes, and a Community regulation to cover social security for self-employed migrants. The present discriminations in this area against third-country migrants need to be progressively eliminated in so far as this is administratively possible (which it may not be in all cases with regard to the exportability of benefits to the country of origin).

Another major problem area for migrants is housing. Here, as in the case of the handicapped, there is a case for using the expertise acquired by the E.C.S.C. in the housing field to promote and help to finance housing projects to meet the special needs of migrants. An important scheme of this kind has been carried out in the working-class area of Kreuzberg in West Berlin, where there is a high concentration of Turkish workers.

The improvement of living and working conditions for migrants is bound to be a slow and piecemeal process, where the role of the Community institutions is likely to be secondary to that of national authorities and institutions such as the trade unions, whose role in the integration of migrants is crucial. Whether the process would be greatly helped by the Community's adoption of a formal Charter for Migrants, setting out their rights, is problematic. The Parliament has asked for such a charter, and it could be useful; but too much reliance should not be put on it. In a sense the most important step that could be taken would be to give migrants the political right of participating in elections. At present this right exists only for Commonwealth and Irish immigrants in the United Kingdom. There is a strong case for eventually giving all E.E.C. citizens the right to vote in elections in their host country if they are living and working abroad (perhaps as an optional alternative to retaining the vote in their home country to avoid giving the migrant a dual vote). Whether this right should be extended to third-country migrants is much more questionable. After all, many of them come from countries which do not allow their citizens the right to vote at home. But there is a case for giving third-country migrants too some form of political expression at *local* level. For it is at this level that the issues of discrimination and the provision of basic services are important. If the migrant had a political voice at this level it would do more to remedy present abuses than any kind of assistance or pressure, however well meaning, from national governments or *a fortiori* Community institutions.

To add to the complexities of the migrant questions there is the un-palatable fact that a substantial proportion — probably around 10% — of the migrants currently in the E.E.C. are there illegally. They may have entered illegally or they may have remained behind illegally after their initial work permit expired — moving to another employer, maybe to another E.E.C. country, and passing out of the ken of the authorities. The illegal migrant is of course highly vulnerable. He cannot claim social security or assert his rights against his employer if necessary; he cannot claim education for his children; he is eminently exploitable.

What can be done about this problem? The trade unions have argued from time to time that the contract hiring of labour should be a State monopoly, as it already is in some Community countries — or that any private employment agencies should be subject to very stringent control. The aim is to stop the "trafficking in human flesh" which they believe some such agencies practise — particularly, though not exclusively, through the hiring of illegal immigrants. But there is no great support for such a rad-ical move which would *inter alia* (unless the law was very carefully drafted) render illegal secretarial agencies, executive "head-hunters" and the like.

The Commission's alternative has been to propose a directive which would levy heavy fines on any employer convicted of knowingly employing an illegal migrant; though how one could prove that he did so knowingly is not easy to assess. At the time of writing the situation remains obscure.

The illegal immigrant has acquired special significance in the light of the very dramatic change in the attitude of the E.E.C. countries towards third-country immigration during 1974. With the onset of the recession all the big labour-importing countries — West Germany, France, the Benelux countries — imposed a virtually total ban on immigration from third countries and, in general, refused to renew the work permits of existing migrants as they expired. The expectation was that there would be a fairly swift reduction in the total number of third-country migrants in the Community which would both ease the social problems of integration and — more urgently — liberate more jobs for the indigenous workless. In fact the wastage was much less than anticipated. A much larger number of migrants than had been expected simply "went illegal". This fact has helped to explode one of the persistent myths about Community migration. It had been argued on both sides that there was a fundamental difference between the British and Continental situations in that immigrants to the United Kingdom (other than the Irish, whose situation is unique) came to settle, whereas the gastarbeiter on the Continent came to do a job for a limited duration with the firm intention of returning home as soon as possible. (This was one reason why the Continental host countries on the whole saw no necessity for spending large sums of money on integrating migrant families into the society around them.) It is now clear, however, that a large number of third-country migrants also have come to the Community to settle there and have no intention of going home again if they can avoid it — especially when the chances of getting a work permit to return to their present host country once they leave it are poor. Once this is accepted, the whole question of immigration and of the assimilation of migrants takes on a new dimension. The problem facing the Continental countries is much more like that facing the United Kingdom than either had thought.

More urgent than the issues of integration and assimilation, however, is the question of what kind of immigration policy the Community is going to adopt towards the cluster of Mediterranean countries from whence the bulk of the third-country migrants come (at least to the original Six; in the British Isles and Denmark the issues are a little different, as we shall see). For it is clear that it will be neither equitable nor possible to maintain the present (1976) ban on immigration from these countries very much longer. Equally it is clear that it will not be practicable to return to the pre-recession "open-door" policy of virtually unrestricted immigration — not for social reasons but because of the gloomy employment forecasts indicated in the previous chapter. And, given the fact that the E.E.C. is becoming increasingly a unified labour market (at least so far as its Continental members are concerned — the United Kingdom and Ireland, being islands, can insulate their labour markets rather more easily from the others if they wish), it is not practical for individual member-States to "go it alone" in immigration policy with the kind of bilateral deals which Germany and France, for example, have struck with individual third countries in the past.

Why can the ban on immigration not be maintained? In the first place because the Mediterranean labour-exporting countries cannot (with the possible exception of Greece) hope to find enough jobs at home even for their existing workers, let alone for a reflux of migrants; nor can their economies do without the remittances the migrants sent home. Over the years a pattern of labour movement has developed in Europe which met the needs both of the labour-hungry and of the labour-surplus States. To break that pattern now is to impose enormous burdens on a group of countries ill-equipped to bear them.

They are also countries which, for one reason or another, the Community can hardly afford to see founder. Nearly all of them are potential members of the E.E.C. Greece has formally applied for membership, Portugal has announced her intention of doing so; Spain clearly will not be far behind. Turkey has a Treaty of Association with the E.E.C. which is currently being renewed. The Maghreb countries of North Africa, especially Algeria, have special relationships with France. Only Yugoslavia has no special claims on the Community. But the Community can hardly wish to see an economically rebuffed Yugoslavia forced back into the arms of Russia and the Comecon.

All these Mediterranean countries combine weak economies with a shaky social structure and a delicate political balance. Greece and Portugal have emerged recently from totalitarianism of the Right, and Portugal has narrowly avoided a totalitarianism of the Left. Her democracy is precarious and fragile, burdened with a massive payments deficit, heavy unemployment and a huge influx of refugees from Angola and Mozambique. Turkey has a queue of over a million workers who have applied to work in West Germany, and for whom there are virtually no work opportunities at home. For Turkey the reopening of the Community borders is a vital economic and political issue. And she has legal claims on the Community in this respect which, though ambiguous, cannot be brushed aside. (The Turks claim that the Treaty of Association gives Turks the right to enter the Community in search of work; the Community's lawyers that it gives them the right to come only if they have already been offered a job. This is a piquant example of the way in which in the E.E.C. system major political issues resolve themselves into legal squabbles over the meaning of texts.) Where Portugal is today, Spain could be tomorrow. The perilous journey from dictatorship to democracy which Portugal started in 1974 is just beginning, two years later, in her bigger neighbour.

For political, military and humanitarian reasons, the Community cannot abdicate responsibility for these outposts of the third world on its doorstep. It cannot ignore the fact that most of these countries are seeking, or will shortly seek, eventual membership of the Community — with the right to absolute freedom of movement which this entails. The Community has always maintained that it is open to any European country to join it provided that it is a democracy. It will be hard therefore to exclude these aspirants.

Therefore there must be, sooner or later, a Community policy on immigration. Such a policy must reflect the needs of the Mediterranean countries and the job opportunities open in the Community. It needs, therefore, an underpinning of employment forecasting of the kind discussed in the last chapter. Indeed, if there were no other reason for a system of labour market forecasts, it would be needed as a basis for a credible E.E.C. immigration policy. The policy must also reflect the ability and willingness of the importing countries to meet the social needs of the migrants and their families.

As always, there are complications. The United Kingdom has the special problems of Commonwealth citizens, and France has rather similar relationships and commitments with many of her former possessions. Denmark enjoys reciprocal free movement of labour with the other Nordic countries outside the E.E.C. So any Community immigration policy is likely to be shot through with special clauses and exemptions. The evolution of a full-scale co-ordination of policy in this area is likely to be, for this and other reasons, slow. But a start can be made by creating a Community standard form of bilateral agreement between member-States and third countries, and establishing minimum standard provisions concerning commitments made or to be made by the Community (for example in association agreements or commercial agreements with third countries). This could be accompanied by the regular evaluation, perhaps twice-yearly, of labour supply and demand throughout the Community (monitored perhaps by the Standing Committee on Employment), and by the gradual extension to third-country migrants already in the Community of equality of living and working conditions, and particularly the right to be accompanied by their families and to transfer wages and savings to their country of origin. Finally, there could be a renewed attempt to end the abuses arising from activities of certain kinds of employment agencies and other organisations which batten on illegal immigrants.

This whole complex of issues concerning migration is one of the most difficult facing the Community, embracing as it does many interrelated problems. Not least is the issue posed at the beginning of this chapter: How can one reconcile the principle of free movement of labour, and the need to humanise it, with the principle of achieving a more even spread of activity both within the Community and between the Community and its neighbours? What, in other words, is the contribution which can be made to social and economic policy by regional development?

The Role of Regionalism

We should never lose sight of the fact that, while many people will always want to migrate in search of better opportunities, a fuller life, or sheer curiosity and a sense of adventure, *forced* migration is a social evil however much it can be humanised. So a long-term policy for migration must seek above all to reduce the need for it.

It is generally accepted that the Community has done too little about this in the past. Moreover, regional problems have become more acute with the enlargement of the Community from six members to nine. Among the original Six, only Italy had serious regional problems. Of the three new members, two have important regional needs (and even Denmark has the special problem of Greenland, an area of regional deprivation if there ever was one). So the regional dimension has become larger with the enlargement of the E.E.C., and will become progressively more so with any subsequent enlargement.

The establishment of the Regional Fund is a recognition, albeit grudging, of this. But a Fund is not a policy. The Fund will help to divert some development, which might otherwise have gone elsewhere, to a region in difficulty. It will accelerate certain projects which might otherwise not have happened so quickly, or in a few cases not at all. But its overall impact, like that of the Social Fund, will be marginal. For we all know that the causes of regional deprivation are complex and that much has to do with the quality of the environment and of life generally — especially in the decaying industrial areas which typify the British regional problem and which are different in almost every way from the agricultural regions of underdevelopment in southern Italy and the Irish republic.

What is needed, therefore, is not just the provision of Community money but a multi-disciplinary attempt to identify what are the causes of the vicious cycle of regional deprivation and how they can be put right. A look at regional policy from this angle — and it makes little difference from this point of view whether the region is inside the Community or outside it — would link such a policy much more closely with social policy, on the one hand, and industrial policy, on the other. On the social side, the role of housing as well as that of vocational training would be an important area for examination and possible action. There would also be clear links with the kind of actions being undertaken in the poverty programmes described in Chapter 7. On the industrial side it would be necessary to identify the many factors involved in decisions on the location of industry and the various aids and restrictions imposed by national and sub-national authorities. One would hope that in its next phase Community regional policy would seek to develop this comprehensive approach, and thus integrate itself much more firmly into the mainstream of Community decision-making. For only when that has been done, so that regional development becomes one of the guiding principles of Europe's economic policy rather than an afterthought, will the issues of migration begin to admit of a solution. But that day, I am afraid, is still far off.

CHAPTER 5

Participation and Industrial Democracy

Given its provenance, it is not surprising that one of the three principles of the 1974 social action programme should have been the development of more effective participation of the social partners in Community decision-making and of workers in the life of the enterprise. It is clear that only by a more meaningful process of participative decision-making could the Community attract the loyalty and enthusiasm of those groups who felt, rightly or wrongly, that they had gained too little from economic integration to date.

In fact it had always been intended that employers and workers should play a major part in the "making of Europe". When the E.C.S.C. High Authority was set up in Luxembourg, care was taken to see that, so far as possible, the three groups — civil servants, businessmen and trade unionists — were equally represented on the staff. The E.C.S.C. Consultative Committee was tripartite, and there were tripartite advisory committees for various aspects (e.g. health and safety) of E.C.S.C. work in the two industries concerned.

Unfortunately this principle was not followed in the staffing of the E.E.C. Commission, which from the start was much more dominated by officials from national governments. It is true that one of the two consultative bodies in the E.E.C. structure — the other being the Parliament — explicitly involved the social partners. The Economic and Social Committee is divided into three groups, each of which functions to some extent independently. The first group consists of employer representatives of the nine member-States, the second trade unionists, while the third is made up of independent experts and representatives of other interest groups such as consumers. But the "Ecosoc", as it is called, is a cumbrous body which has never exercised as much influence on Community decision-making as its founders hoped — partly because its work very largely duplicates that of the European Parliament.

Over the years substantial lobbies have established themselves in Brussels to look after the interests of particular interest groups. The trade unions in particular have established strong links with the social affairs directorate-general of the Commission, just as at national level links between trade unions and ministries of labour or employment are normal. But, just as at national level, the unions have found that the key decisions affecting workers are often made in other departments — so that if one wants to have a real influence on policy, links with one department are not enough. In the United Kingdom the desire for greater involvement in the central field of economic policy-making led in the 1960s to the establishment of the so-called "Neddy" system — the tripartite National Economic Development Council and its offshoots at sector level, the Economic Development Committees or E.D.C.s. Similar systems, of one kind or another, exist in most of the other E.E.C. countries (France is probably the main exception).

Similarly, at Community level there has been pressure from both employer and union organisations for closer involvement in E.E.C. decision-making across the board, and a similar objection to being fobbed off with special access to one department alone. This pressure has grown as the social partner organisations have been adjusted to the integration process. So long as they were only organised at national level it was not easy for employers or unions to demand special privileges in consultation at *European* level. However, in the early 1970s on both sides there was a move to develop European-wide organisations which could speak with the Commission, the Parliament and the Council of Ministers on an equal basis.

Thus the trade unions created after the enlargement of the E.E.C. a European Trade Union Congress (E.T.U.C.), which grouped together practically all the important unions in Western Europe (extending, in fact, well beyond the E.E.C.). The main bodies excluded from the E.T.U.C. at the time of writing in late 1976 are the French C.G.T. (Communist) and C.F.D.T. (left-wing Catholic) unions, as well as the so-called *cadre*, or white-collar, unions in certain countries. The fact that the Italian Communist union, the C.G.I.L., is a member means that the E.T.U.C. spans the political spectrum of the European labour movement and embraces a clear majority of trade unionists in all E.E.C. states except France. This means that for the first time the European trade unions, as to the overwhelming majority, can speak on E.E.C. affairs with a single, articulated voice.

On the employers' side the same process has been at work, though less dramatically. At the time of writing there are three main employer groups at E.E.C. level — the U.N.I.C.E. representing the private sector, the C.E.E.P. representing the public sector and the C.O.P.A. representing agriculture. Since these three groups in practice work closely together, the employers' fragmentation does not put them at a serious disadvantage *vis-à-vis* the unions.

These groups are represented on a whole series of advisory committees covering different aspects of the Commission's work — vocational training, free movement of workers, health and safety, the Social Fund and so on. Perhaps most important of all is the Standing Committee on Employment, which has already been mentioned. In addition, at sector level there has been a growth of so-called "joint committees" — groups of employers and unions meeting together, under Commission chairmanship and with a Commission secretariat, to discuss matters of common interest.

It has been the objective of both the unions and the Commission to expand the number of these committees, which currently cover some ten industries, and to broaden their terms of reference. Hitherto most of the committees have confined themselves to considering such matters as health and safety provisions, the impact of E.E.C. regulations, and occasionally certain aspects of fringe benefits which are of general interest. The trade unions have made little secret of the fact that they would like to see these joint committees developing into European-wide collective bargaining agencies, and also as agencies empowered to carry out structural planning at E.E.C. level. The Commission has given certain signs of approval of this ambition, but has done little to implement it in the face of strong opposition from employers; and the employers' continued opposition to such a move has in fact greatly slowed down the process of incorporation of these committees.

Employer suspicion, based on the fear of European-wide collective bargaining, also imposed a brake on the setting-up during the 1974 - 6 recession of sector groups, reporting to the Standing Committee on

Employment, to keep under review employment prospects in particular industries and to provide a basis for detailed manpower planning at European level. Such committees would clearly enable Community institutions and governments to understand and respond better to employment trends. But the employers feared that the proposed sector groups would somehow get merged with the joint committees, and what had begun as a fact-finding exercise would end up as a piece of collective bargaining machinery.

My own view is that talk of "European collective bargaining" at this stage is a red herring, and that the unions have been foolish not to admit this publicly; for by their reticence they have encouraged employer phobias which have got in the way of consultation in areas which are of genuine common interest and importance — on the one hand, matters of health, safety and standards; on the other, issues of economic develop-ment including, most importantly, jobs. I believe that the unions them-selves are not ready, given the considerable and widening divergencies of living standards between member-States, to envisage European collective bargaining in any meaningful sense. Nor does the Commission have any interest in trying to force an unwilling partner to the bargaining table when there are so many more urgent matters to discuss.

I would like to see the present pattern of consultation based on the Standing Committee on Employment developed into the kind of dialogue which in the United Kingdom takes place in the "Neddy" forum. This would require the regular attendance of ministers of finance as well as of labour instead of occasionally, as hitherto. It would mean that economic policy as well as jobs should be regularly on the agenda. It would mean the development of sector groups roughly analogous to E.D.C.s ("little Neddies") in the United Kingdom. Whether the existing joint committees should be absorbed in these sector groups is a matter which could be settled on a case-by-case basis. I would also like to see, as indicated in Chapter 3, the Community's existing instruments for boosting employment (hopefully reformed and rationalised) put under the supervision of this Committee — not from the point of view of detailed management but from the viewpoint of deciding priorities.

While this would go a long way towards meeting the demands of the social partners for greater participation in Community decision-making, there is another bit of machinery to be considered also in this context. In

1974 the Commission set up a special "social partners bureau" attached to the office of the President to establish regular consultation with the social partners on those aspects of policy which lay outside the social field; for example, regional development, commercial policy, overseas aid, and so on. I regard this as an important development which the Commission should develop further. Almost all policies have a social dimension which has not always been taken adequately into account in the past. What the exact links should be between an expanded bureau and an expanded Standing Committee on Employment is a matter for discussion. But clearly there should be such links, at least at the Commission level.

So much, then, for the participation of the social partners in Community decision-making. But "participation" has a second aspect — the aspect of industrial democracy within the enterprise. This too has an important role to play in the present phase of Community social policy.

Industrial democracy has three aspects which need to be considered here. (A fourth, often bracketed with them, will be discussed in Chapter 8 — that is asset formation, or profit-sharing.) There is the issue of participation of worker representatives on decision-making bodies such as boards of directors (in German, *Mitbestimmung*). There is the question of humanising and democratising the workplace. And there is the question of labour law to protect the worker.

Let us start with the issue of *Mitbestimmung* — not because it is in my view the most important, but because it is the one in which the Community institutions have had the longest involvement and the one which has attracted the most attention.

In its pursuit of measures to harmonise competitive conditions, the Commission has prepared over the years a number of directives on the reform and harmonisation of company law in the nine countries. The process of debate on these directives in the Parliament, the Economic and Social Committee and the Council of Ministers has been exceptionally protracted. The most widely publicised and important of these draft directives has been the Fifth Directive, which proposed *inter alia* the adoption of a system of two-tier boards of directors on the German model, separating the supervisory from the executive board functions, with statutory provision for the representation of worker interests on the supervisory board.

The origin of the Fifth Directive is a little curious. It began around the end of the 1960s when European opinion was alarmed at the prospect of the progressive take-over of the European industrial structure by U.S. multinational companies. A very influential book by the French publicist Jean-Jacques Servan-Schreiber, entitled *Le Défi Américain* ("The American Challenge"), had argued that Europe was in process of being colonised by U.S. industry — simply because U.S. firms were taking advantage of the economies of scale created by a European Common Market and the Europeans themselves were not. If Europe wanted to compete with America on its home ground, therefore, Europeans would have to create multinationals on the U.S. scale. This meant that there would have to be cross-frontier mergers within E.E.C. industry on a much greater scale than heretofore. The main obstacles to such mergers were thought to lie in the difficulty of reconciling different national company legislations.

So the idea gained currency of creating an E.E.C. alternative to national company legislations — the so-called "European company", which would be incorporated under a European company law statute to be created. Then, if a German company wished to merge with an Italian or a French one, they could jointly decide to opt out of their respective national legal systems and incorporate themselves as a "European company" (*Societas Europaea*). The problem then was simply to draw up a draft statute for a European company which would be an option available to any enterprise wishing to opt out of national company legislation. Clearly the European company law statute should not be more favourable to companies in its general provisions than the average of national legislation, for if so one risked a stampede out of national legislative systems which could cause domestic embarrassments.

The problem was particularly acute for West Germany, which at this time was the one E.E.C. country whose legislation required companies above a certain size to reserve a third of the seats on their supervisory boards to worker representatives. If the *Societas Europaea*, the German Government feared, did not have broadly similar provisions there could be a mass exodus out of German company law into European company law, and the German Government would have some difficulties with its unions as a result. So from the outset the draft statute for the European company was linked to a "German model" which provided for a two-tier board and worker representation at board level.

After numerous vicissitudes, the draft statute for the *Societas Europaea* arrived on the desks of the Council of Ministers for decision at the end of 1975. Its structure bears a strong resemblance to existing German company law structures, and the probability is that few companies will avail themselves of the option. For in the meantime the enthusiasm for European mergers, and the fear of U.S. domination, have greatly diminished.

Having got itself involved in the issue of company law reform and worker participation almost by accident, however, the Commission found itself in the early 1970s dragged further and further down the road. The European company was seen as an interim solution only to the problems posed in *Le Défi Américain*. Was it not necessary in the long term, in order to equalise competitive conditions, to aim for a complete harmonisation of company law throughout the Community? And should this harmonisation programme not include provisions for board structures?

So the Commission produced, in 1972, its famous draft Fifth Directive, which proposed a harmonisation of company board systems on the lines of the European company. It was no accident that the Fifth Directive mirrors closely the German model of company structure, for most of those concerned with this area of E.E.C. activities happened to be Germans, the German Government and unions had a particular interest in the extension of their system, and they were able to argue with some cogency that their model had certainly worked in its home country.

At the same time, the model posed a great number of difficulties, particularly for those countries which did not have a two-tier system in their company law. It was one thing to envisage such a radical departure from existing patterns in most of the Community countries for a purely optional facility like the European company, which nobody need adopt if they do not want to. It was much more serious to contemplate overturning existing national company legislations for the sake of imposing changes regarded as highly controversial.

As the debate went on, the focus subtly changed. The economic or administrative convenience of harmonising legislation began to recede somewhat into the background as people became increasingly aware of the major social implications of the changes proposed. The major issues came to be seen as being the need to involve the workers through their representatives more fully in the running of business (the "industrial democracy" argument), and to make business more responsive to its broader responsibilities in society (the "social responsibility" argument). Most people could accept the objectives; but there was no consensus on the desirability of the means chosen to achieve them.

On the *participation* question, there was division in trade union ranks. In those countries where there was a high degree of social cohesion, with strong moderate trade union movements—Germany, the Netherlands, Denmark — there was strong union support for worker representation at board level. But in Italy and France the dominant trade unions, Marxist in ideology, rejected it as a device for linking them to the capitalist system. Their model for trade union activity remained one of confrontation rather than co-operation.

The attitude of the British, Irish and Belgian unions was midway between that of the Germans and that of the Latins. They were in favour — though not unanimously so — of worker participation on boards. But they did not see this in any way as altering their objectives or strategies but rather as an extra weapon for pursuing them. Thus they would use seats on boards as a collective bargaining instrument; they would both have their cake and eat it. Thus, in contrast to the German ideology, they saw the accountability of worker directors as being limited to the promotion of their constituents' interests; they would not have the same accountability as other directors. Second, again in contrast to the Germans, their representatives would be appointed by the trade unions and not directly elected from the shop floor.

The attitudes of employers and governments tended to mirror that of the unions. In Germany, Denmark and the Netherlands (as also in Sweden, Norway and Austria) governments tended to favour, and employers to acquiesce in, worker participation at board level. In France employer groups remained implacably opposed, and government hesitated. In Italy the subject hardly figured in public debate. In the United Kingdom and Ireland employers objected strongly to the interpretation put on worker participation by their unions, and the whole issue was a subject for intense debate.

The other main matter of contention was the concept of a two-tier board which raised grave issues of principle both for British and Irish company law. With the enlargement of the Community this issue became more rather than less difficult to resolve.

By 1974 it had become clear that there was no basis for a Community-wide consensus on the Fifth Directive, neither among the unions, the employers or at government level. The German model, on which the Fifth Directive was based, was unsaleable as it stood to countries like the United Kingdom and France with radically different systems and traditions. On the other hand, the subject could not simply be dropped, for during the years since it had first been mooted the importance of improving the social accountability of business, and of broadening the base of industrial democracy to give workers more say in the operation of the business system, had demonstrably grown. "Participation" could not be taken off the European agenda whatever the difficulties of implementation.

The Commission therefore decided to try to do two things. First, it prepared a discussion document, a so-called "Green Paper" on the British model, which set out the objectives to be sought in worker participation at board level and in the separation of supervisory and executive functions, and then examined the various paths which could be followed to achieve these objectives. In short, without abandoning the principles of the Fifth Directive, it subtly moved away from concentration on a single model for realising them. It envisaged relatively lengthy transition periods for those countries whose legal systems or traditions rendered adjustment to a German-type system particularly hard, during which alternative approaches to a formal two-tier board and to worker representation could be canvassed and experimented with, to see if they would meet the Commission's conditions. A much more flexible, less doctrinaire approach with much more leeway for experiment but with a clear objective at the end of the road, distinguished the Green Paper — published in 1975 — from the Fifth Directive. The Green Paper envisages a public debate, which looks likely to continue for some years, before the Commission will be in a position to draw the threads together, hopefully arrive at a new consensus and draw up further proposals for harmonisation to replace the Fifth Directive.

This seems an eminently sensible approach, for we are dealing here with a far from static situation. The position is changing in most of the E.E.C. countries with the exception of Italy, where the whole subject apparently attracts minimal interest or support. In France the Sudreau

Committee in 1975 published a report which sought to move France much nearer to the German position of *Mitbestimmung*. The government was still considering it in late-1976. In the United Kingdom the Bullock Committee was due to report at the end of 1976 on the formal establishment of worker participation. In Germany a great debate has been in progress on the increase of worker participation from one-third to one-half of the seats on supervisory boards. Whatever might have been a consensus in the early 1970s, when the Fifth Directive first appeared, is unlikely to represent one in the late 1970s when the Commission will presumably draw up its revised version.

The second approach taken by the Commission in view of the impasse on the Fifth Directive was to look more closely at other avenues for participation. It has long been argued by industrial experts that the place where industrial democracy can be most meaningful is not the boardroom but the shopfloor. It is perfectly possible for a company with trade unionists on its board of directors to be highly autocratic and hierarchical, and for one with no such directors to be extremely open, democratic and participative. This is because channels of communication upwards and downwards in an enterprise, and similarly within a trade union structure, can be highly ineffective. In West Germany there have been many criticisms that once trade unionists become directors they lose touch with their members — and indeed the German convention specifies that a worker-director has the same obligations to shareholders and other company "stakeholders" as do other directors, and that he should not give special preference to the interests of the workers.

So it is at least equally important to have "direct" as "indirect" industrial democracy. By "indirect democracy" is meant the representation of worker interests in the decision-making process. By "direct democracy" is meant procedures which give the individual workers a direct say in the structure of their jobs and working conditions. This can be done to a certain degree by a structure of works committees such as are increasingly common in British industry, or *comités d'entreprise* in France. In some countries these committees are given specific rights, for example of consultation of certain kinds of investment or job restructuring.

Many employers find this kind of structure, in contrast to worker participation at board level, much more meaningful in terms of improving worker motivation and productivity and in easing the tensions of industrial relations. Trade unions tend to be wary of them in some cases as tending to blur the conflictual role of the unions in enhancing worker interests through the traditional collective bargaining process.

Nevertheless, the importance of shop-floor democracy is increasing. The Sudreau report mentioned above lays great stress on the need to give the worker more autonomy in his or her work. In Norway and Sweden much effort has been devoted since the early 1970s to experiments on restructuring work to make it less boring and demeaning, through the development of autonomous work groups or other means which give the worker more responsibility in his work and a greater say in how it is carried out. These experiments have been supervised in Norway by a tripartite control group representing unions, employers and the autonomous Work Research Unit. In Sweden there have been many such experiments, notably in mass-assembly line industries, of which Volvo's Kalmar car plant which went on stream in 1974 has been perhaps the best publicised to date.

It is not surprising that the Scandinavian countries should have pioneered experiments in work humanisation in Western Europe. Scandinavia does not have a large population of migrant workers willing to do the unattractive, boring, repetitive jobs which indigenous people shun. Moreover, Scandinavian workers almost certainly have a higher standard of education than other European workers. In consequence, it has been much harder to persuade Scandinavians to accept boring, repetitive jobs such as those in assembly-line industries, and such industries have experienced growing problems of absenteeism, high turnover and declining product quality as educational standards (and therefore expectations) rise. Thus Volvo, for example, has been prepared to spend large sums of money at Kalmar to introduce an alternative technology for car-making to the assembly line, which is almost certainly less technically efficient in orthodox terms but which no less certainly scores heavily on worker satisfaction.

Many of the E.E.C. countries are following the Scandinavian lead. Germany has a massive government-backed programme of action research and experiment in the work humanisation field. Britain has its own much more modest Work Research Unit, with a tripartite governing body. For all the Community countries sense a growing concern among their peoples with the quality of working life, a growing demand for higher standards of health, safety, ergonomics and job satisfaction, a growing resistance to authoritarianism at all levels. These demands are part of the "revolution of rising expectations" in Europe's work-force, of which the pressures of wage inflation are another manifestation. They cannot be ignored. As educational standards rise, and as the role of the migrants in Europe's labour force declines, they will almost certainly become more acute. The turbulence of the last few years could be a portent of worse to come, unless action is taken soon to defuse the tensions.

It was at French insistence that a phrase about the "organisation of tasks" was written into the priorities section of the Community's social action programme in January 1974, and it was the French who pressed most strongly for the setting-up of a European Foundation for Improvement of the Environment and Living and Working Conditions which would focus initially on promoting measures of work humanisation. This Foundation, with the same tripartite management structure as the European Vocational Training Centre, was set up in Dublin at the beginning of 1976. Its first task is to act as a centre for information on work humanisation experiments and to promote action research. How it will develop is unclear. Important though the subject is, it is one which it is hard for governments or governmental agencies to influence directly to any great extent. Solutions will depend to an overwhelming extent on the climate and culture within individual enterprises.

Nevertheless, what can be done at Community level — however limited — should be done; for this is an essential part of the "human face" of Europe to which the Community has committed itself. And it is easy to sympathise with the special concern of French governments, facing a social situation which in their country is full of menace, where the normal warning signals provided by a strong trade union movement do not operate, and where a return to the sudden catastrophic eruption of May 1968 cannot be altogether excluded.

Mention should be made here of another institution proposed in the Community social action programme, though not yet operational — a European Trade Union Institute financed by the Community, to enable the trade unions to train and equip their members for the new responsibilities which participation in its various forms will impose on them. I believe this is important, and I regret the delay in its establishment; for lack of enough trained people in the trade union ranks could constitute one of the biggest bottlenecks in the move to greater industrial democracy in Western Europe.

The other main plank in industrial democracy is the strengthening of the rights of workers through a framework of labour law designed above all to promote job security. Some E.E.C. countries, such as West Germany, have long had a rather comprehensive framework of labour law. Denmark has been able to achieve a high degree of job security through collective bargaining procedures which have the force of law. In the United Kingdom, by contrast, until the early 1970s there was very little by way of labour law — though, as a result of the 1974 social contract between the Labour Government and the T.U.C., a labour law framework covering such issues as redundancy, trade union recognition, bargaining procedures, non-discrimination on sex or other grounds and dismisssal procedures is being hastily constructed.

The case for Community involvement in labour law is a dual one — the need to equalise competitive conditions (on the rather dubious ground that a company subject to stringent labour law provisions is at a disadvantage *vis-à-vis* one not so subject), and the much more important "social" argument concerning the need for a better quality of working life and more participation. The first is an argument deriving from the Treaty of Rome, the second from a political judgement on Europe's priorities.

In fact, given the divergencies in standards between the Nine, it is not feasible in this area, any more than in the case of social benefits, to achieve complete equalisation. All that the Community can do through its labour law directives is to establish a basis, a set of minimum conditions, on which individual countries and enterprises can and should improve. There were two such directives in the 1974 - 6 social action programme as well as the recommendation on the 40-hour week and 4 weeks' holiday. The first directive established minimum procedures and compensation for collective dismissals which were due to reasons other than misconduct on the workers' part. This was approved in 1974, and was to be followed by proposals for the harmonisation of national legislation covering procedures for *individual* dismissals. The second directive, still unapproved at the time of writing, was designed to ensure that when the ownership of an enterprise changed hands the new owner took over responsibility for the totality of rights and privileges negotiated by his predecessor with the workers. In other words, such rights could not be nullified by a change in ownership.

It is a moot point whether the Community should seek to go much further in building up a corpus of E.E.C. labour law. What has been done already or is in the pipeline, together with the provisions of the women's and migrants' programmes seeking to outlaw discrimination, represent quite a significant input. The problems of reconciling different national systems are very formidable.

But perhaps something more could be done in the special case of multi-national companies. The attitude of the Community institutions towards multinationals has been highly schizophrenic. On the one hand, the institutions have tended to reflect trade union phobias about the power and irresponsibility of multinationals and the destabilising effects of their capital movements around the world. On the other hand, there has been an awareness of the need for the capital investment and the technical know-how which, properly treated, the multinationals can bring to Europe. And there has been a continuing uncertainty as to whether one can, or should, discriminate in favour of E.E.C.-based multinationals against U.S. and other foreign-owned ones. As a result of these unresolved contradictions the E.E.C.'s stance has been confused and ineffective.

My own view is that the attitude of the Community towards multi-national companies should on the whole be a welcoming one subject to acceptance of the codes of practice drawn up by the O.E.C.D. But I think it is not unreasonable to ask, in advance of any more general company law provisions, that multinationals should be required to set up, where their workers wish, European-wide works councils to which they should report — perhaps at six-monthly intervals — on the overall progress and plans of their companies. I believe such a move would dissipate much of the present fear and hostility towards multinationals in Europe.

There is also a need (and measures to this effect have been in the pipeline an unconscionable time) to establish formulae for the reconciliation of conflicting national labour laws which affect those working in other Community countries than their own — whether as migrant workers or as *frontalliers*—(those who cross national frontiers daily to go to work). And there will no doubt be other issues thrown up to Community level by the restless pressure throughout Europe for a better deal between employers and workers, which is likely to remain a feature of our turbulent times. The Community institutions have to continue to be responsive to these movements, though the power of legislation to deal satisfactorily with them is perforce limited.

CHAPTER 6

The Social Budget

For many years certain people in Brussels have had a dream — a dream that somewhere along the highway leading from the Common Market to a federal United States of Europe the route would lie through the harmonisation of social systems. One of the many difficulties in the realisation of this dream was the almost complete lack of a data-base at the Community's disposal concerning the details of the existing national systems. It was to remedy this, and thus to provide material on which future decisions regarding the scope for harmonisation could be based, that the Commission proposed as part of the 1974 - 6 social action programme the establishment of what was called the First European Social Budget.

The Social Budget is not in fact a budget in any normal sense. It is simply a factual comparative statement of expenditures by the nine member-States in certain social fields for the years 1970 - 5. Its limitations are important. It excludes capital expenditure and it concentrates on expenditure to cover the following risks or needs: sickness, old age, death, survivors, invalidity, employment injuries and occupational diseases, unemployment, family needs (including maternity) — as well as various miscellaneous categories of spending (to cover such things as physical or mental infirmity, natural catastrophes, etc.). It thus leaves out of account a very wide range of social spending, such as housing, education, training, public health institutions and so on.

The first draft of the 1970 - 5 Social Budget was presented to the Council of Ministers in December 1974. The projections for 1975 were based on economic assumptions (on prices, earnings, employment levels) made during the first half of 1973; they had therefore been largely invalidated by inflation. It was thus necessary to revise the 1975 figures substantially, and the revised Budget was not submitted to the Council until March 1976.

Even as a partial snapshot of the social spending field, the Social Budget provides a wealth of revealing information — on demographic trends, on differing national priorities, on the different methods of financing social protection in the different countries. In certain countries, for example, a substantial part of social benefits are levied from employers and employees; in others, the overwhelming majority comes out of general taxation. In some countries the provision of benefits is much more selective than in others. Catholic countries tend to give a much greater weight to family allowances than do Protestant countries. The German social welfare system still shows significant traces of the nineteenth-century ethic of work orientation on the basis of which it originated, while the French reflects the Napoleonic ideal of strengthening the peasant families from which France's armies were traditionally recruited. The British system still strongly reflects, despite the relative poverty of the nation today, the generous "universality" principles of the postwar welfare state inspired by Lord Beveridge.

At the same time, the relative scale of benefits clearly reflects the relative wealth of nations. The United Kingdom comes badly out of the exercise, for example, in comparison with Denmark or West Germany. That is hardly surprising. But in all countries the proportion of social spending to gross national product or to total national income has been growing significantly. This has been particularly true of the richer countries such as Denmark, Germany, Luxembourg and the Netherlands.

A number of questions arise at this stage. First, if the Social Budget is to give a meaningful picture of social spending across-the-board in the nine countries, its scope needs to be broadened from current spending on social protection to include capital spending, and certain currently excluded categories of social spending such as vocational training and housing. This will give rise to technical problems, for in these spheres the officials concerned will no longer be able to rely, as they can in the field of social protection, on the E.E.C. social accounts.

Second, even in its present limited form the Social Budget tends to reinforce the impression of enormous diversity throughout the Nine and the extraordinary difficulty — and doubtful desirability — of achieving a harmonised E.E.C. social system. The diversity is of two kinds. On the one hand, it is hardly surprising that the richer countries have, by and large, more advanced systems of social welfare than the poorer. Can there in these circumstances be an upwards harmonisation of social systems without either a transfer of resources from the rich to the poor countries or a freezing or slowing-down in the advance of welfare systems in the rich countries? And would either of these be acceptable to the rich countries at the present time?

The other element of diversity in national systems is a reflection, not of different levels of national income, but of differences in history, culture and value systems. Some of these differences have been hinted at above. It would be very hard, and of doubtful value, for the Community to try to iron out all these variations which reflect the vagaries of historical development and to seek to impose on the whole E.E.C. a standardised social system which would in fact satisfy nobody.

However, this does not mean that the Social Budget has only negative value. For in fact it serves two purposes which to my mind are of great value. First, it serves to highlight some of the major issues preoccupying — or which ought to be preoccupying — the policy planners at national level. In each of the member-States of the Community social welfare systems have been developed since the war on the back of continued economic growth. They have been part of the national dividend from such growth. In all spheres — social protection, education, housing, health — there has been a continuous and on the whole little-planned growth in spending year by year. Such spending has been little related to other trends — to movements in demography, to changes in standards of living or consumer spending patterns and so on. Spending in the social field has been much influenced by the relative strengths of the ministers responsible for particular spheres and by the power of the pressure groups concerned (doctors, teachers, etc.). Debates on priorities have tended to concern themselves with short-term marginal changes — a little more for housing this year as opposed to health, the balance to be made good next year, and so on. Now, as a result of this process, a situation has been reached in all the nine countries where the proportion of national income going to the public sector is a cause of concern, and where social spending as a component of public spending has to be contained. These pressures are at least as strong in rich countries like Denmark and the Netherlands as in relatively poor countries like the United Kingdom and Ireland.

What is needed in each country is a more rational system of allocating social spending according to priorities, to replace the annual horse-trading between politicians which tends to be the present preferred system of national "social planning". And in the establishment of such a critique for relating social spending to needs and means, the Social Budget provides an invaluable base for discussion between the member-governments, and the Community institutions an invaluable catalyst for enabling governments to benefit from the collective wisdom of the Nine in solving problems of general interest and importance.

But the Social Budget has another function too. It is to help identify those areas where there might be scope for selective harmonisation of social benefits and where particular categories of people are in need. Since 1975 the director-generals responsible for social protection in the nine national governments meet regularly with the Commission to exchange views. Out of these discussions the Commission has been able to distill certain specific areas of social protection which seem to lend themselves to a Community approach, and a draft directive for the harmonisation of certain categories of social protection is now (end-1976) on the stocks. This is the first venture of the Community into this field — a relatively modest one, but it could be the harbinger of others in years to come.

In short, therefore, harmonisation in the social field should not be totally excluded. But it cannot be on the basis of harmonisation for harmonisation's sake, and it must take account of the very real and important differences in social structures within the Nine. It must proceed on the basis of identification of needs and the establishment of minimum standards consistent with the civilised, compassionate society the European Community aspires to be. The migrants, as already indicated, form a clearly recognisable category of people for whom Community action to assure minimum social protection is both necessary and, in principle, acceptable at national level. Other special categories — including particular categories of self-employed — are also coming to be recognised as falling within the same rubric; and doubtless the list will be extended in future, as standards rise and the habit of policy co-ordination and the practice of Community research develop. But the process is likely to be a pragmatic, piecemeal one for as far ahead as one can see. The idea of a "Social Union", widely discussed and canvassed in the early 1970s, seems to recede further the more its complexities are explored.

In addition to the Social Budget there is a need to strengthen the statistical resources available to the Community in other ways. The need to strengthen statistics in many areas — on employment and the labour market, on migrant workers and their families, on incomes and assets, on industrial accidents and safety, and elsewhere — is a recurring theme throughout the social action programme. In particular, there is a need to extend the programme of Community ''social indicators'' in order to understand better the felt needs of the European peoples in the social field. Such indicators fall into two categories. On the one hand, there are the ''objective'' indicators — those indices of welfare which can be quantitatively assessed (''welfare'' in this context meaning both material standards, and what might be called ''happiness'' standards, as measured by such things as the rate of crime, divorce, suicide, industrial unrest and so on). On the other hand, there are the ''qualitative'' indicators which record people's attitudes — to work, to leisure, to their neighbours, and so on. The Commission has made considerable progress — though not yet enough — in developing a network of social indicators, which should help to provide an on-going guide to the way Europeans actually feel about their social structures and about the priorities for social advance. Without such information — however imprecise and sketchy it may be in the initial stages — we shall be groping in the dark in our efforts to articulate social strategies for Europe.

Even more than in other parts of the social action programme, it is clear that in those aspects of social policy covered in this chapter we are just at the start of a long and probably bumpy road. But in the long run it can be even more important for Europe than the areas covered in earlier chapters, which in one form or another are limited to workers and labour relations. Given its origin as an instrument for economic integration, it is not surprising that it should have been in the area of work and employment that the Community made its first moves into the social policy field. But social policy is not just about jobs. It is about life and sooner or later the scope of European social policy must move out from the factory to the home. The next chapter will indicate some of the areas in which this is already happening and the possible scope for further such advances.

CHAPTER 7

Poverty, Health and the Environment

The first concern of social policy is with the disadvantaged. Many of these disadvantages appear at the place of work. The actions of the Community in favour of women, the young unemployed and the workers in regions and industrial sectors in trouble come into this category. Actions on behalf of the migrants cover disadvantages at work and disadvantages in the home (that is to say, in the communities where they and their families live). The same is true of the handicapped. In the first stages of the social action programme the Community institutions dealt with those whose disablement was not so severe as to exclude them permanently from normal work. But the Commission also has a commitment within the social action programme to prepare before the end of 1976 proposals for the betterment of life for the more severely handicapped — those working in sheltered workshops and those unable to work systematically at all. In this programme the Commission is no doubt considering proposals in the field of vocational training, housing policy (the Commission's housing department has been subsidising research into the housing needs of the handicapped as it has for migrants), social services and health provision.

The Community institutions have also, as we have seen, begun to look tentatively at ways in which the national provision of social protection for particularly disadvantaged groups can be improved. But it is an observable fact in all European countries that there are certain categories of people trapped in situations of acute poverty and deprivation for whom the services of the welfare state do not seem able to provide a solution. These pockets of poverty in our rich, materialistic societies are a phenomenon of growing concern. These people are the involuntary ''drop-outs'' from society, excluded and seemingly unable to reintegrate themselves in it. Whether they are excluded because they are poor or poor because they are excluded, the fact is that they are caught in a vicious circle.

Sometimes these "excluded groups" consist of special categories of people, such as one-parent families; sometimes of groups living in a particular area, like the decaying centres of certain big cities suffering from bad housing, bad environmental conditions, bad schools and too few jobs. The problems in any case are common to all member-States of the Community, and there is a common interest in finding solutions (and a knowledge bred of common experience that solutions cannot be found through the normal forms of protection given in national welfare state systems).

So there has been a wide measure of support for the Commission's proposal in the social action programme to mount a two-year experimental anti-poverty programme, taking a number of case studies chosen from each of the member-States, and working with a steering committee consisting not only of government officials but also of representatives of voluntary welfare organisations from each of the nine States. The pilot projects were agreed and the programme launched in mid-1975. At German insistence the budget was limited to about $6 million, all to be spent by the end of 1976. Since many of the projects will not be completed by then, and since the Commission and most of the member-States had envisaged the programme as having a continuing life — the first programme being in fact a pilot venture for what might well be a much larger and more ambitious exercise subsequently — it seems clear that there will have to be a debate in the Council of Ministers on the next stage during 1977.

Within the context of the overall question of poverty, the Commission has also published studies on the special problems of old people. But the old do not seem to be a high political priority in the depressed conditions of the mid-1970s; their hardships, so often suffered in secret and silence, do not command the same attention as those of more vociferous, better organised groups.

Mention has already been made of the concern with *industrial health and safety* in the original E.C.S.C. programme. One of the first provisions of the social action programme in 1974 was to extend the same tripartite network of consultative committees which had been used to monitor research into health and safety questions in the coal and steel industries and to make recommendations for government action, where appropriate, to the broader canvas of industries covered by the

Treaty of Rome. A consultative committee on Industrial Health and Safety covering the whole of E.E.C. industry, excluding the extractive industries (which were absorbed into an expanded Mines Safety Committee), was accordingly set up, and held its first meetings in 1975. Its first task, still under study as I write, is to establish a working programme on priorities within its immense field.

The guidelines prepared by the Commission envisage a triple function for the committee. On the one hand, there will be a continuing role in a number of across-the-board issues such as training, research, statistics and the like. At the same time it will need to concern itself with particular sectors of danger or difficulty where there is a particular recognised industrial health hazard calling for Community action or a particular group of workers at special risk (migrants, for example). Over and above this, however, there is the question of harmonisation of regulations for products and processes. The Community has a twofold interest in this. First, it has to ensure that national standards and specifications are not being used as a device for concealed protection against imports from other E.E.C. countries. Second, it has to see that the specifications conform to Community health-and-safety criteria. Clearly it is not always easy to marry the two interests. Clearly, too, it is much easier to get agreement on Community standards *a priori* rather than *a posteriori* — before, rather than after, commitments have been made at national level. So an effective "early warning" system is required to enable the Community institutions to express a view before firm commitments are made at national level on new standards or specifications for products and processes traded within the Community.

It is also clear that there will be a growing link between questions of safety and those of work humanisation and industrial democracy. In the coal and steel industries the Community has an ergonomics programme of research, and one of the issues before the General Safety Committee is the question of the role of trade unions at shop-floor level in safety questions. Should joint committees on safety within the enterprise be established, and what powers should they have? Should they, for example, have the right to order a cessation of production, if they are not satisfied that conditions are fully safe, over the heads of the management? These are issues of growing concern on which decisions will need to be taken at Community level at some point.

The Commission has taken a particular interest for some time, deriving from experience acquired in the E.E.S.C., in industrial diseases. And more recently there has been a growing interest within the nine member-States in the co-ordination of certain aspects of medical research and in common action on certain emerging health problems — for example the problems of drug addiction, ''social'' diseases caused by bad environmental conditions, stress conditions and so on. There are now regular meetings at E.E.C. level of those concerned with national medical research programmes designed to avoid duplication of effort, to relate the Community's own research programme to national programmes and priorities, and to facilitate the exchange of information and ideas. There are also, less frequent, meetings under Community auspices of national medical officers of health to look at issues of common concern at policy-making level (on the lines of the meetings, already described, of those concerned at national level with employment policy or with social protection). This is another instance of the catalytic role played by the Commission in areas of common interest but where there is no strong commitment to harmonisation under the Treaty.

There has been some discussion over the last few years on the possibility, or desirability, of the Community making a more formal move into the field of *public health* — of whether there is enough commonality of interest among the Nine to justify a Community action programme on health such as already exists on environmental pollution, on industrial safety and in many other areas of social policy. This seems to be quite a likely development at some point in the next few years if the current process of evolution is allowed to develop unchecked. The analogy with the poverty programme, with rehabilitation of the disabled, with the co-ordination of policies in the fields of employment policy and forecasting, with vocational training, with work humanisation, with consultation on social protection matters, is a strong one. These are all areas where the Community member-States have identified issues of common concern which justify regular exchanges of views and information, where certain specific problems requiring a common approach have been identified, and where the Commission is able to play an important role as a catalyst.

Public health seems to conform to this pattern. It is clear that an E.E.C. public health programme would be a selective, pragmatic one, concentrating on clearly identified issues of common interest. The scope for directives or for sweeping harmonisation proposals is likely to be limited. On the central issue of public health organisation there seems no way in which, for example, the distinctive British approach exemplified in the National Health Service can be reconciled with the normal Continental approach to health services, which relies much more on national health insurance schemes rather than a State-run medical and hospital service. Nor does there seem any pressing reason to do so. But that, however we organise ourselves in the health field, we can learn from each other, and that we face common problems to which we are more likely to find solutions by working together rather than in isolation, seems indisputable.

One area with important health implications has long been a Community concern. This is the field of *environmental pollution*. Since 1958 Euratom (now merged with the European Community) has had a specific responsibility for radiation protection and the control of nuclear emissions, as well as for the general safety of nuclear reactors. No nuclear power station can be built in the E.E.C. without Community approval on safety standards.

During the present phase of Community activity the Commission, which has taken over Euratom's responsibilities in this field with the merger of the different Communities, has been concerned with the revision of basic radiation protection standards, with proposals to reduce the risk from electromagnetic rays and from exposure to ionizing radiation (especially from certain consumer goods and in medical applications), and with preparing the ground for a longer-term programme in biology and health protection through agreement on basic norms in key areas.

However, during the early 1970s in response to growing public concern about pollution and environmental deterioration, the Community broadened its concern to embrace a comprehensive programme of environmental protection. This was a major aspect of the "new deal" sanctioned at the 1972 summit conference. An environmental programme was prepared in parallel with the social action programme, and a series of directives to reduce pollution from noxious materials are currently (1976) making their way through the Community institutions. The technique has been to establish criteria for harmful effects, for example in drinking water and in the use of lead. The Commission's programme envisages a number of directives dealing with various potentially lethal substances emitted into air or water, and to establish tolerable noise levels. Progress in this area is slow, not because there is dispute about the need for proper control of pollutants, but because of the technical problems arising from the limited data available for sampling, on which directives in this field must be based. There are also problems arising from the divided responsibility for environmental control at national level (in Italy, for example, ten different ministries are involved), and from the fact that physical conditions of wind and water-flow vary substantially from one country to another — with the result that a build-up of pollutants which can be a serious threat in one country may readily be dispersed by natural forces in another. In such cases the country which does not see an immediate risk is disinclined to impose on its industries the considerable extra cost which may be involved in meeting Community standards. Allied to this is the problem that pollutants are highly mobile, so that the country producing the pollutants may not be the one that suffers their effects. The Community's principle is that "the polluter pays", but it is not always easy to translate this into practice.

A long-term environmental programme is clearly a massive undertaking. It involves the establishment of clean air, clean water (both fresh and sea), the removal of wastes, the establishment of reasonable noise ceilings, effective control of products with possibly dangerous side-effects on the ecology, a reasonable balance of land use, conservation of natural resources, protection of wild life (for example, Europe's migratory birds annually butchered in Italy), provision of facilities for leisure activities and the humanisation of the working environment. Within this vast field the Community has to decide, as in the social field, what are those aspects which have a Community dimension (which must of course include anything which involves the "export" of pollutants across national frontiers), what are the priorities for action and what is the appropriate means in each case.

The problem about the use of directives is, as already indicated, the lack as yet in many cases of an adequate data-base on which legislative standards can be erected. Unfortunately the willingness of governments and industries to face the cost involved in meeting environmental standards has diminished with the recession and the squeeze on profit margins, and in some cases trade unions — sensing that jobs may be at risk if extra costs are imposed on industry — have also become luke-warm. The easiest way to resist change is to challenge the statistics on which the proposals for directives are based — and in the nature of the case the statistics are challengeable. So the fight for a better environment will be a long one.

There is one issue which has, however, been thrown into particularly sharp focus by recent events. In order to reduce its dependence on oil, the E.E.C. is embarking on a major programme of nuclear construction. It is evident that this programme arouses considerable misgivings among many people on the grounds of environmental and public health risks. This is an area of genuine concern on which the facts are elusive. The Commission contains within itself, through its incorporation of Euratom, a strong "pro-nuclear" lobby. This group tends to discount the risks inherent in an accelerated nuclear programme. They may well be right. But it would be better for all concerned if the issues were faced openly, and if there could be a public debate on the matter. For besides the risk of a nuclear breakdown all other current environmental problems seem minor.

Questions of health and environmental control are not the central stuff of day-to-day policy-making nor are they the central issues of social policy at the present time. But they are of great importance for the long-term development of European society and the quality of life therein. And they are for the most part questions which have a European as well as a national dimension. I would hope therefore that the Commission would in future find ways of devoting more resources to their solution. It might, for example, be desirable to consider setting up a special directorate-general in Luxembourg to deal with all questions of health, safety and the environment (including all aspects of nuclear safety), with some kind of "ombudsman" attached to it, to reassure the citizens of the Community that their future safety was being kept under constant review in the nuclear programme and was not lost in the interstices of an often face-less and introverted bureaucracy.

CHAPTER 8

Inflation and Social Justice

It can be argued that the two great social challenges facing Europe today are inflation and unemployment — and that of the two, inflation is the more serious. There are many explanations for the great inflationary wave which hit all Western industrial societies at the end of the 1960s; but clearly one of the most important elements was the rise in expectations at almost all levels of society, and impatience at the failure of the economic system to meet these expectations.

The postwar industrial boom in Europe had many side-effects. It spelt the death-knell of traditional beliefs in social hierarchy. It marked the end of the traditional pattern of Christian society, which tolerated very marked inequalities in rewards in this life on the assumption that these inequalities would somehow be rectified in the after-life which Christians implicitly believed would follow death. In this expectation people could afford to be patient. But with the decline in traditional religious belief the tolerance of inequality sharply diminished. At the same time the boom brought a genuinely more fluid society in which some people from very humble origins were able to "make it to the top" (especially in the worlds of sport, entertainment, pop music and fashion, in certain aspects of distribution, finance and property development), and their well-publicised success stories have served as an inspiration and a stimulus for others too. And, at least equally important, the mass media with increasing effectiveness and persistence have spread the gospel of materialism to almost every household in the Western world, encouraging people to want and to demand an ever-increasing living standard. In the days before television the ambitions and aspirations of most people were limited to what they could see in their immediate vicinity. A man's ambition was to live a little better than his father or his neighbour; he did not aspire to the life-style of the gentry because he had little direct knowledge of it.

Those days are gone for ever. Today all but the very poorest families in Western Europe can see clearly how the rich live, and they are encouraged and enjoined to seek the same kind of life. We live, as Marshall McLuhan has aptly put it, in a "global electronic village". Society is no longer divided into opaque partitions. People today in all European countries want the good things of life, and they want them now because, by and large, they no longer believe they will get a second chance.

So, in the sphere of material aspirations as in the sphere of sexual morality, modern technology has irretrievably altered the balance of society, removing certain inhibitions or restraints and creating new temptations, new opportunities. Cost inflation is the analogue of the permissive society. And modern technology has also made society as a whole increasingly vulnerable to pressure from particular sections of people who operate vital parts of the productive process. So the ability of such groups — many, but by no means all of them, organised into trade unions — to increase their share of the national "cake" has considerably increased as society has become more capital-intensive and more technologically complex.

This is not to say that the present inflation derives exclusively from pressures of greed or personal aggrandisement within our societies. The readiness of governments to meet their commitments by printing money rather than paying their way; the sharp rise in commodity prices — notably, but not only, oil prices; the growth in Western economies of non-productive publicly financed activities at the expense of the productive sector: all these have played a part. But the most important element — certainly so far as Europe is concerned — has been the revolution of rising expectations and the inability of governments to contain the resulting pressures.

I make no value judgements on where the blame for this situation is to be apportioned, or whether present-day society is better or worse in its general quality of life than the society we had in what now seems an age away, in the mid-1960s. But it is clear that inflation has caused some major problems in our societies. First, the expectations have demonstrably outrun the ability of our economic systems, at current levels of technology, to meet them even in favourable market conditions. Wage demands throughout Western Europe, before the 1974 recession, were running at 20 - 25% on average. The maximum feasible real annual increase in gross national product for E.E.C. countries at current technology levels is around 5 - 6%. This leaves an inflationary gap of around 15 - 20% which can only be filled by rising prices or the erosion of profits. This is a crude mathematical summary of the inflationary problem facing Western Europe in the period just before the 1974 recession.

From this a number of consequences follow. If profits shrink, the ability of industry to expand to meet the demands placed on it is curtailed. If prices rise, the wishes of those seeking real improvements in living standards from income rises are frustrated. This leads to social friction and to an escalation of money demands as people come to discount future price rises. The vicious inflationary spiral starts. And the authority of the State, and of the established institutions of society, is diminished because in the last analysis this authority, at least in democratic societies, rests on the belief that they can and will ensure social justice. Once this belief goes, one can expect a sharp decline in standards of law and order and social cohesion, and a growing tendency for individuals and groups to grab what they can out of the melée on the grounds that if they do not look after themselves nobody else will.

This situation has not been basically altered by the recession which replaced the boom in 1974, and which was in large measure the direct result of the inflation. Certainly inflation rates have been coming down; but so have the productive increases needed to meet the demands which sparked off the inflation in the first place. The gap between expectations and achievement remains unbridged. And the fact that inflation rates have been declining much faster in some E.E.C. countries than in others has created a new destabilising factor in the Community, because of its effects on relative balances of payments.

So nobody can be certain whether, as production picks up again and unused resources in the Community are put back to work, inflation will start to rise again. If it does, our situation is parlous. But if we are to avoid it, action needs to be taken now to re-establish the equilibrium and the cohesion in our societies which inflation has at least temporarily disrupted.

The Community's social action programme can be fairly criticised for the scant attention it pays to this overriding problem. It is of course true that inflation, like unemployment, is an *economic* problem, and that it cannot be cured without effective governmental policies on the management of demand, the control of the money supply and the allocation of resources between the public and the private sector. But it is also true that it is a *social* problem — not only in the sense that it creates major problems of social injustice, but that its solution demands measures to restore the balance between different sections of society and the cohesion without which modern society cannot function; and, by the same token, measures to restore respect for the institutions by which we are governed.

Inevitably, therefore, one is led in the direction of what in Britain has come to be called, unoriginally, the "social contract". By the social contract is meant a broad agreement between the main elements of society — the social partners, in particular the trade unions — and the government, which will in a sense seek to replace the traditional cements provided for society, in the form of accepted religion-based ideas of social order and hierarchy, with a new cement, based on a broad agreement on the proper ordering of society to replace the "free-for-all" which has generated a self-defeating inflation.

One element of a social contract clearly has to be a consensus on the amount of income rises which the economy can sustain. For such a consensus to have any force it must be accompanied by broad agreement as to how income rises should be distributed — and in practice (if not in theory) by some measures to match wage restraint by restraint on prices and profit margins. But it almost certainly has to go wider than that. If union leaders are voluntarily to forgo part of their bargaining power — and no social contract which does not involve such a voluntary renunciation is likely to mean very much — they will certainly demand certain assurances in return. Such assurances are likely to concern the broad distribution of resources in the economy, the broad thrust of government economic and social policy (including the allocation of public spending), the "social wage" (i.e. supplements to private spending which come out of the public purse, such as social security benefits and the like), and matters affecting the distribution of power in industry (labour law and worker participation questions). In short, the social contract is in essence a deal in which pressure groups such as trade unions accept a constraint on collective bargaining freedoms in return for a greater say on the way the country is run. They bargain money in the short term for power and influence, in the expectation that in the long run a better-run economy can produce more real wealth for all.

Most E.E.C. countries today have analogues to the British social contract. France is a partial exception, mainly because of the weakness and fragmentation of the unions in that country. In Italy the weakest party has tended to be the government, with the result that the prime agents in the social contract have tended to be the employers *(Confindustria)* and the unions combining at national level. In the Benelux countries, in West Germany and Denmark (as elsewhere in Scandinavia) the trend to consensus government has gone very far — and in Germany in particular it has been very successful in holding the rate of wage inflation significantly below other E.E.C. countries.

Clearly, therefore, there is a link between economic measures to control inflation and social measures to extend the scope of participation and industrial democracy, and to protect the victims of past inflation. Social justice, in other words, is both one of the weapons in the anti-inflationary armoury and a prize to be regained from the defeat of inflation.

Thus many aspects of the community's social action programme could be said to be part of a comprehensive anti-inflation policy. Certainly it is wrong to look at social programmes purely as cost items, to be encouraged in boom times but cut back when times are hard. This is wrong-headed from several points of view. It is when times are hard that social spending is particularly needed; and if social measures are seen as an alternative to inflationary wage demands, they may produce an immediate economic as well as a socio/political pay-off. (This is to say nothing of those aspects of social spending like vocational training which positively promote employment.) At the same time it is clear that when spending cuts are necessary social programmes cannot be sacrosanct. At times it may be necessary to hold back social spending in favour of investment in industry, for example (as in the United Kingdom in 1976 - 7). So from time to time the focus of social spending may need to change with economic circumstances.

What is the role of the Community in all this? It is certainly premature at this stage to envisage a Community-wide ''social contract''. At the same time, if national governments are moving in this direction one would hope and expect that Community social measures would reflect the trend and not run counter to it. Moreover, in so far as consultations on employment questions at Community level between governments and social partners are developing, and look like moving into what I have called on the British analogy a "Neddy-type" pattern, involving broad issues of economic policy co-ordination as well as more mundane questions of labour policy, it seems logical that the dialogue should extend to "social contract" issues of incomes policy and social priorities. This seems a useful and desirable trend, and one would hope that in framing its social policy proposals the Commission would bear it in mind.

At the same time, the problems of reconciling the conflicting interests and approaches of governments in this field are very great. This was seen in the Commission's abortive attempt in 1974, following a request from the Council of Ministers, to establish a Community consensus on wage indexation, both as a measure of social justice and as a device for taking the expectations element out of inflation. The Commission reviewed existing policies on indexation in the Nine, tried to draw some conclusions from the success or failure of various systems, and proposed some tentative conclusions. But the subject was too hot for the Council of Ministers to handle, and the issue was dropped.

Nevertheless, in the social action programme the Commission has a mandate to carry out similar exercises (comparison of current national situations, leading to possible proposals for Community action) in three related fields: minimum wages, the "dynamisation" (i.e. indexing to cost of living, and/or to gross national product) of pension schemes, and asset formation (or profit-sharing) schemes.

A paper on asset formation was presented to the tripartite conference of finance and labour ministers and social partners in mid-1976. At the time of writing, work is still going on on the other two. Asset formation has acquired a considerable importance as a subject in the present situation. National schemes to channel part of industry's profits into trade union funds, to be re-invested in industry, look at first glance like a relatively painless way of (a) syphoning off part of wage demands into non-inflationary channels; (b) transferring part of the ownership of industry into hands of workers; (c) giving workers a postponed wage increase through the dividends on the funds re-invested in industry; (d) assuring industry of adequate funds for capital renewal and expansion; (e) at the same time, acquiring for the public authorities through the unions a substantial measure of control over the distribution of capital to industry. That seems a remarkable number of birds to kill with one stone.

Measures of this kind are under consideration or on the statute book in Germany, Denmark and the Netherlands (and, on a much more limited scale, in France). Many countries also operate savings schemes designed to encourage home ownership. And, of course, many enterprises have operated profit-sharing schemes for a good many years, with varying degrees of success in identifying the workers with the success of the business.

The question really is whether the idea of a government-sponsored system of asset formation on the proposed Danish or German model is going to succeed (the Germans have postponed the issue until the economic climate improves, while the Danish Government has been hesitating for some years), and whether other governments are likely to take it up. The idea of an "investment wage" — in other words, the freezing of some part of wage increases in funds compulsorily reinvested in industry — is an attractive one at a time of wage inflation and capital shortage. But will it be acceptable to the workers and will they accept the risk element inherent in all capital investment? Similarly, the idea of extending ownership and control over substantial parts of industry may be attractive to unions and to left-wing governments. But will it lead to unacceptable distortions of the capital market and to interference with the freedom of enterprises to operate commercially? What is the relationship of this issue to that of *Mitbestimmung*?

The whole subject is fraught with complexity, and it would certainly be useful for the E.E.C institutions to keep a watching brief on the situation as it evolves country by country. But any decision at this stage on what would be the right policy for the E.E.C. as a collectivity or on possible harmonisation measures, would almost certainly be premature. One guesses that the same conclusion would be drawn on the other subjects pending in this area — minimum wage schemes and "dynamisation" of pensions.

The important point, however, is that the Community institutions should be studying, on a regular on-going basis, the various elements that could go into a package embracing anti-inflation measures and measures to promote social justice — in other words, which could form part of a social contract. For it is clear that it is down this road that the E.E.C countries will need to go if inflation is to be contained and social cohesion restored within a democratic framework. For some time at least they will need to travel separately, given the differences in social structures and in the institutional frameworks. But at some stage the paths may converge, given the centripetal forces within the Community and the extent to which the social partners are already locked into discussion of economic and social issues with governments at Community level. The Community institutions need to be ready to react when this point is reached and to ensure that in the meantime the paths taken do not mean that eventual convergence will be more difficult than it needs to be.

CHAPTER 9

The Unsolved Problems

The preceding chapters have attempted to provide a snapshot of E.E.C. social policy as it stood towards the end of 1976. Before trying to evaluate the effectiveness and the relevance of the policy to Europe's needs, it is worth mentioning two policies which were in the original drafts of the programme but which were dropped because of political opposition. The first was turned down by the Commission itself; the second found its way into the programme but was not implemented through lack of support at the Council of Ministers.

Both measures concerned income maintenance for the unemployed. The first proposal was an ambitious scheme for Community unemployment benefits. If this had been approved it would have been the first step towards the Europeanisation of social benefits — to "social union" in other words. The justification for the proposal was that the process of integration is a factor in the creation of unemployment in certain sectors; this after all is the reason for Article 4 of the European Social Fund. There is therefore a stronger case for transferring unemployment benefits, in whole or in part, from national to Community level than there is for other benefits. Also, since the worst unemployment problems tend to arise in the poorer countries, who are least able to pay generous benefits, a Community system for unemployment benefits would be a step towards equalising incomes throughout the Community, and thus helping the poorer countries to meet the burdens of economic and monetary union.

The idea was that the Community should establish an unemployment fund which could be used to "top up" national schemes. Thus the countries with the least generous national schemes would make the biggest drawings on the fund. Eventually the hope was that national schemes would gradually be merged into the Community fund, so that at the end of the day the E.E.C. institutions would be funding all un-employment benefits throughout the Community.

The opposition to the scheme centred on the unwillingness of the richer countries to contemplate the transfer of wealth across national frontiers which was implicit in the proposal, and also the sacrifice of national sovereignty which would be required if the level of unemployment benefit ceased to be a national and became instead a European responsibility. There was a very real fear that the richer countries would be held back by the need to level up the benefits for the poorer countries. But there were other difficulties as well. Was it meaningful to think in terms of a single level of payment throughout the Community, when living costs and other benefits varied so much from country to country? Moreover, countries with generous systems would be penalised, and there would be a strong temptation for national governments to economise on national benefits and leave the Community to make up the difference. Finally, how would one incorporate into the system redundancy pay-ments by firms?

If there had been agreement on the principle, the formidable admin-istrative complexities could doubtless have been ironed out. But there was, and is, no such agreement. It is clear that the Community is not yet ready for the harmonisation of social systems or for the extension of Community financing into this area.

The second measure also concerned income maintenance for un-employed workers. The problem is that workers undergoing retraining, whether under the Social Fund or through other means, face a substantial loss of income. The Social Fund cannot be used for purposes other than training or movement costs. It can neither finance the capital costs of training establishments nor income maintenance for those being trained. The same problem arises in most retraining schemes at national level. So the social action programme proposed that member-States should commit themselves to introduce adequate income maintenance for workers during retraining and subsequent job search; and that the Com-munity itself should undertake support towards the cost of income maintenance linked with development of E.E.C. employment targets as discussed in Chapter 3. This would of course have required a new Community fund outside the Social Fund.

This proposal, shadowy though it was, attracted a good deal of support from Italy and Ireland. In Italy the State-run redundancy fund, which in certain circumstances takes over responsibility for paying workers who would otherwise be made redundant while they search for other jobs (a process which may or may not involve retraining), has had great difficulty in meeting all the demands on it since 1974. Some form of E.E.C. assistance to the fund would ease Italy's problems considerably. The United Kingdom has subsequently established a similar structure though on a smaller scale.

Establishment of such a Community capability would also help to meet one of the defects of the Social Fund which was identified in Chapter 3. We saw there that the Fund has difficulties at a time of general recession because in such times it is hard to identify growth industries for which workers from declining industries can be retrained. There is therefore a strong argument for using the Social Fund, or whatever other instrument is available, for "training for stock" — deliberately creating a pool of skills for which outlets may not immediately be available, on the grounds that in so doing one is creating a capital asset for the future (at the risk of a "brain drain" in the meantime), besides helping the workers concerned to improve their long-term prospects.

For this to be a feasible proposition two things are required. First there needs to be an adequate system of manpower forecasts so that long-term opportunities can be discerned and so far as possible quantified. Second, there needs to be provision for a system of income maintenance to sustain the workers who are being "trained for stock" until the appropriate jobs materialise.

I would certainly hope that as and when the Social and Regional Fund are restructured and hopefully merged into a new E.E.C. Employment Fund — as suggested in Chapter 3 — this new Fund would have the power to support national schemes for income maintenance based on a framework of Community manpower planning. There would be strong support for such a move today from Italy, Ireland and probably the United Kingdom. But one should not underestimate the opposition to be expected from Germany, and probably France and the Benelux countries — not against the principle but against the scale of resources which would be needed for such a fund to be effective.

We come here to the first and most fundamental of the problems confronting E.E.C. social policy. This is the question of the amount of resources to be spent at Community level on social questions. At present social and regional spending — concentrated mainly in the Social and Regional Funds — account between them for a little over 10% of the Community's annual budget of some $9 billion. More than three-quarters of the total is consumed by the common agricultural policy. This division of resources does not reflect any Community decision on priorities either at the level of the Commission or of the Council of Ministers. It arises because the different types of expenditure are committed in quite different ways. Agricultural commitments are in a real sense uncontrolled — in the sense that once ministers of agriculture meeting together in Brussels or Luxembourg have agreed on the support prices to be paid for individual agricultural products, the Community is obliged to pay these prices irrespective of the level of production. So the Community never knows what the cost of its agricultural policy is going to be. Once prices are fixed, the budget will be a function of the weather and farmers' productivity — both incalculable.

By contrast, of course, the Funds at the Community's disposal have to be budgeted each year, and the total amount to be allocated to each has to be decided by the Council of Ministers in consultation with the European Parliament on a proposal by the Commission. This is a highly unsatisfactory procedure, for it means that the Commission is not in a position to decide rationally on the different priorities for its expenditure, nor can the Council and Parliament debate the Community budget with a full knowledge of the different options available. We shall have to come back to this question of the formation of the Community budget in the next chapter.

Any discussion of the budget is, however, bound — in the social and regional sphere — to resolve itself into a tussle between the rich and the poor countries. Whether one is debating the size of the Social and Regional Funds, or the scope for harmonisation of social benefits, the fundamental question is how much the rich countries are prepared to contribute towards the poor. Since this is the fundamental question at stake in the matter of European social policy, it would be desirable for it to be openly debated in the future so that everybody knows where he or she stands. At present the budget procedures, for the reasons stated above, do not permit the question to be openly posed. So I am tempted to say that before one can draw up the next stage of Community social policy in a meaningful way, one has first to reform the budget procedures of the Community in such a way that the Commission is obliged to form a public judgement on the way it wishes to spend its money and the amounts which will be required, and then to defend this judgement before the Parliament and the Council of Ministers. Only when this degree of clarity is achieved will it be possible to determine how much political room for manoeuvre exists in the development of those aspects of Community social policy which cost money.

During the past few years the Commission has found itself trapped, in the social policy field, between Scylla and Charybdis. On the one hand, the trade unions and the governments of the poorer countries (Italy and Ireland, and less systematically the United Kingdom) have argued that the social action programme had been outdated by the recession and should be fundamentally restructured to concentrate much more heavily on ways of helping to cope with unemployment, and that adequate resources should be provided for a fundamental attack on unemployment. On the other hand, the richer countries, who constitute a permanent majority in the Council of Ministers, have made it very clear that they will not provide the kind of means which would enable such a fundamental attack to be mounted — that they would indeed prefer the social action programme to focus on measures which could be carried out with no extra expenditure whatever.

There is of course an easy argument in reply to the criticism that the social action programme has been outdated by the recession. It is to ask the critics what elements in the programme they would abandon. The social action programme is designed to help the under-privileged. The lot of the under-privileged does not become any easier in a recession; it becomes worse. Given the enormously long time-scales involved in getting policies through the Council of Ministers, it is simply not feasible to chop and change the programme every 6 or 12 months because we are at a different point on the business cycle. So if the critics are not asking for anything to be dropped, but for more to be added, the answer has to be that in present (1975 - 6) circumstances there is simply no majority in the Council of Ministers to support them. This is of course not to say that future programmes should not try to be more ambitious, and to take into account the lessons and the disappointments of 1974 - 6.

The point has already been made that the 1974 - 6 social action programme was a compromise between a number of different objectives, and that it reflected a consensus view on what was politically possible. In looking at the next stage of European social policy it would be sensible to take stock of where we are and of the *scope* of Community social policy so far, the *methods* available, the priority *problems* still to be solved, and the *new issues* emerging in the late 1970s. When we have done this we should be in a position to draw up some provisional guidelines for the future.

On the first point it is clear that up to now the scope of Community social policy has been rather limited in relation to national policies. In *housing* and *education* (considered as a social service) the role has been marginal. In housing, apart from the special E.C.S.C. function, the Community's contribution has been limited to actions in the migrants and handicapped programmes and to a certain amount of research into the role of housing and urban planning in regional development. It is not easy at this point in time to foresee a major expansion at E.E.C. level in this field. Similarly, in education the Community has done little beyond the specific question of education for migrants' children. The Treaty of Rome rather pointedly excludes education from its purview, and there is little disposition on the part of member-governments to envisage harmonisation or Community initiatives in this field.

The situation regarding *health* and *social protection* has been discussed in some detail above. In each case one can, I believe, anticipate an increasing Community involvement in the future, but in each case progress is likely to be piecemeal and pragmatic.

The core of Community involvement in social policy is thus likely to continue for some time to be in the fields of *work* and *employment*. If one takes the three major objectives of the 1974 - 6 programme — full and better employment, improved living and working conditions, increased participation — it is difficult to argue that any of them has ceased to be a major objective. Indeed, full employment has receded since 1974 and its achievement has thus acquired a greater urgency, whereas the other two objectives are by their nature likely to be a permanent element in any social programme. But I think that one could add a fourth major objective to be inscribed in the next stage of European social policy for reasons elaborated in the last chapter — social justice.

Looked at from the viewpoint of social policy as national governments see it, therefore, any E.E.C. social action programme in the present epoch is likely to look rather specialised and lopsided. But there are good reasons for this. The resources at the Community's disposal are limited. It is not a government, nor is it equipped to take over the function of a national government. It is not likely except in special circumstances to be better at problem-solving than national governments, with their much greater resources and greater access to the grass-roots. So the Community institutions must concentrate on those areas where they either have a special responsibility arising out of the Rome or Paris Treaties, or where by general agreement they have a particular role to play.

In trying to assess what circumstances meet these requirements, it is useful to look at the methods or instruments available to the Community institutions. First, there is of course the power of the purse — the use of the money available in the various Community funds. But this, for reasons discussed above, is likely to remain limited unless the Community can win the goodwill of the rich countries who control its budget by demonstrating a capability in other directions.

The second instrument is legislation — the establishment, by agreement with the Council of Ministers, of regulations or directives which have then to be reflected in national legislation. Because of the weak juridical basis for social policy in the E.E.C. — due to the relative silence of the Treaty of Rome on the subject — the scope for directives in the social field will always be somewhat limited, failing a renewal of the "political will" too briefly evident during 1972 and 1973.

These are, one might say, the *hard* weapons in the Community's armoury. They are the ones by which the Community institutions tend to judge their success rating, their virility. But they are not the only ones, nor in the social field are they necessarily the most important or effective. We have talked a lot in this book about the role the Commission has been able to play in the social policy field in recent years as a catalyst, an educator and influencer, a co-ordinator of research, a data-bank and a standard-setter. I would myself prefer to judge the effectiveness of the Commission at least as much (where social policies are concerned) on its acceptability and success in this role as on the number of directives passed or the amount of money spent. For social policy is not just about transferring resources from rich countries to poor countries or the harmonisation of conditions and standards. These are important elements but they are not the totality. It is also about a common approach to problem-solving, about pooling ideas and efforts to overcome defects in the quality of life, about a gradual coming together in the search for a European society which will better meet the needs of all its citizens. In this process a body like the Commission (with its sister institutions, the Parliament and the Economic and Social Committee) has a unique role to play which it should never lose sight of.

The Commission should therefore place itself in the centre of a continuing process of dialogue with the other Community institutions, with member-governments and with the social partners. From this dialogue the priorities for social policy should emerge: both the present problems which might admit of a Community approach (through one or other of the methods outlined above) and the emerging problems which are beginning to concern governments and other interests within the E.E.C. In the social field (the one which concerns us here) the Community institutions should not cut themselves off from other bodies with similar interests — the International Labour Organisation (I.L.O.), the World Health Organisation (W.H.O.), the Council of Europe, O.E.C.D., etc. There is no national patent on the solution of social problems, which tend to be broadly similar in all advanced industrial countries.

The Commission will also need to shed some of the suspicion with which it tends to approach the Council of Ministers, and to rid itself of the adversary relationship which has tended to exist since the days of General de Gaulle. Such an approach may be understandable, though probably unwise, in areas where the Commission has a clear mandate to implement clauses of the Treaty of Rome which are being frustrated by one or more member-governments. There are examples of this kind of situation in the field of social policy, but they are rather exceptional (partly because, as we have seen, the Treaty does not give a strong mandate to social progress). In social policy there is everything to be said, in my view, for an open approach by the Commission to the Council and the other Community institutions.

There is also a strong case for broadening the scope of the dialogue where the social partners are concerned. Indeed, the whole concept of "social partners" probably needs re-evaluation. This is in no way to denigrate the claims of the existing social partners — the unions and employer organisations; I have argued the case in this book for a radical strengthening of the system of participation in policy-making between them and governments at Community level. But there are other important interests which have a voice in social policy whose claims to a hearing should be recognised.

One such group are consumers, who are now represented on a consultative body to advise on the development of E.E.C. consumer protection policy. Another are the voluntary social welfare organisations who have played a major role in the preparation and monitoring of the poverty action programme. A third group are the environmentalists, whose interest in the E.E.C. environmental programme (especially the nuclear aspect) is obvious. Professional women's organisations constitute a fourth important group. Against the opposition of the trade unions, who claimed somewhat unconvincingly to be the best spokesmen for working women, the Commission enlisted professional women's organisations as advisers on the programmes for equal pay and equality of opportunity for women, and it has subsequently set up a special Women's Bureau to monitor progress in this field. But — possibly wrongly — the Commission has not adopted a similar approach in developing the migrants' programme. Migrant organisations have not been systematically consulted.

Another sectional interest, particularly important in Catholic countries, is represented by the network of family organisations grouped together at E.E.C. level in COFACE. In my view this is a section of opinion which the Community would be wise to take seriously. For I believe that questions of family policy could emerge during the next few years as among the most important in the European social field.

There is no doubt that the family as an institution is under great strain at the present time as a result of the great social changes now underway. The permissive society has removed some of the cements which in the past have held families together, as have the rapid movements of people caused by the economic boom and the massive migrations which have been touched on in earlier chapters. Mobility is a challenge to family life. It is not the only one. A highly educated, under-employed generation of young people is likely to be a source of frustration and violence second only to that engendered by an unassimilated immigrant community. The tide of violence and frustration is in any case rising, as we have seen, due to inflation — without the added complications caused by unemployment.

In all these circumstances the restraining influence of parental authority and family loyalties is desperately needed but is not always found. For modern society has been busy taking married women out of the home and into work. In so doing it has been responding to deep and fervently expressed desires on the part of women themselves. The Community's programme to assure equality of opportunity for women at work — part of which has been approved but part is still in the pipeline — will carry this process further. In so doing it will be righting social wrongs but it may also be contributing to the creation of others.

For example, in considering the question of helping women with young children who need more income, there are alternative solutions which produce very different social results. One approach is to provide more *crêches* for the children so that the mother can go out to work. This is the approach favoured by the trade unions and the women's organisations. The alternative is to provide women who want it with a home-care allowance in recognition of the service they are performing in staying at home to look after their children. The two are of course not mutually exclusive. If it can afford to do so, the obviously right approach of society is to provide working mothers with the option — *crêches* and jobs, or home-care allowance instead of a job. But the home-care allowance option is unpopular with women's organisations, who fear a *kinder, kirche, küche* backlash which will force women back into the home and deprive them of the rights at work for which they have fought so hard.

Clearly this would be wrong. But on the other side of the coin there is the problem of the maintenance of the family as the basic unit of Western society. Today's "latchkey" child could only too easily become tomorrow's unemployable. There is growing concern in all European countries with the apparently unsatisfactory results of the huge investment in education which has been made over the last two decades. So I believe that among the new issues with which social policy will have to grapple during the next decade will be how to maintain the stability and cohesion of the family without renouncing the social gains which have been made in recent years.

One can point to other emerging issues also, alongside the unfinished business of the 1974 - 6 social action programme. One such issue clearly is going to be the condition of our inner cities — the problems of urban decay and urban renewal. It seems probable that the follow-up to the poverty programme will have to focus, among other issues, on this problem. Much of the work on the migrants' social problems, and on the issues of regional development, bears on this question too. The future of our cities could well be another of those issues of common concern on which the catalytic role of the Commission might be brought to bear.

What other new issues are likely to emerge at Community level? One might hazard a short list. It would include the rise in violence, questions of land use, privacy and citizens' rights. A European Commission on Human Rights would be a highly desirable addition to Europe's institutional furniture.

If one adds to this hypothetical list of new issues the unfinished business of the 1974 - 6 social action programme and the environmental programme described in earlier chapters, it is clear that the range of social problems confronting the European Community is a formidable one. In tackling them the Community institutions will need to draw on as wide a range of expert advice as possible. It is important that the style employed by the Community in its approach to problems in the social field should be open and participative, not secretive and bureaucratic. In fact the Commission has tended, at least in the last few years, to be much more open in its policy-making than national administrations. This is partly because it recognises the importance of securing a base in the public opinion of the member-States, to sustain it where necessary against the powerful pressures of national governments. Because by its nature it is remote and little-known, it has to involve as many groups and people as possible in its decision-making. It needs to have the possibility at least of appealing over the heads of national governments to the people of Europe, even if such an appeal might be a last resort. Otherwise its influence will be very little once outside the mandate of the Rome Treaty.

So the role of experts and of special interest groups in the making of Community policy in the social and related fields is, and should remain, very considerable. But for this influence to be effective, and for the Commission to be able to play the kind of role indicated in these pages, the relationship between the different Community institutions — the Com-

mission, the Council, the Parliament, the Economic and Social Committee —
has to be clarified. That relationship in recent years has been far from
satisfactory. So in the final chapter we need to look first at this relationship
as a preliminary to drawing conclusions on the role of European social
policy in the years ahead.

CHAPTER 10

The Way Ahead

For some time now the institutions of the European Community have been in a state of crisis. The crisis arises from a number of factors. As we have seen, the process of European integration has got bogged down at a halfway stage which satisfies nobody. The original mandate of the Rome Treaty, which gives the institutions of the Community their legitimacy, is losing its force. The main objectives of the Treaty have been realised, but the further stages of integration which were expected to follow after it have not happened, and meantime Europe is faced with new and daunting problems to which the Treaty seems to have little relevance. We have seen this situation at work in the social policy field, but it applies in other areas as well.

In these circumstances what is the European Commission — the guardian of the Treaty and at the same time the appointed agent for integration — to do? Is it to see its role as being the full implementation of the Treaty to the exclusion of other objectives? If the answer is "yes" — and on a strict legal interpretation of its functions it probably would be — then it is doomed to continue to devote its energies to pressing forward with proposals for harmonisation in areas where the political opposition is increasingly greater and the perceived relevance to the real issues of the day increasingly less; to following through the implications of the Treaty in remorseless detail to conclusions which seem to the average European unreal, marginal or both. It thus risks the accusation of sterility and lack of relevance and of being ignored.

For in the last analysis the Commission has little power. All its proposals have to be approved by the Council of Ministers, and the Council is increasingly disinclined to accept measures which may be in the spirit of the Treaty but are not seen to be in the national interest of this or that country. During the 1970s power has visibly been moving from the central Community institutions back to national level. This in my view is only partly because of poor leadership from the Commission. It is also in large measure because the original mandate has gone stale and has not been replaced.

The Commission likes to think of itself as a quasi-government with the prerogatives and the powers of a national government. But it is nothing of the kind, nor can it be. It is not an elected body and it does not have the moral authority of a democratic government. The Commissioners are appointed for four-year terms of office by national governments, so that each Commissioner knows that if he is to have any chance of reappointment after the four years he cannot afford to get too far out of line with his government. So to expect Commissioners to serve Europe exclusively and to ignore the interests of their home country is somewhat idealistic.

Moreover, the Commission lacks the cohesion of a national government. The President neither appoints nor has the power to dismiss or replace his colleagues. He has only a limited influence even in the allocation of their portfolios. Thus he almost totally lacks the power of patronage of a national prime minister.

So the powers of the Commission are strictly circumscribed. In these circumstances there is a tendency for it to stand on its rights, adopt a prickly adversary posture to the Council of Ministers, insist on the rights of initiative conferred in the Rome Treaty and solace itself with the illusion of power to soften the reality of impotence. In these circumstances the safe course clearly is to stay close to the Treaty and not to propose measures in areas where the Treaty is weak or silent.

There is, however, an alternative course, and in my view a better one. It is to accept that the European Community is evolving, that the priorities of yester-year are no longer necessarily the great concerns of today, and to seek to influence and guide the debate which is now going on in the Community about Europe's future. At some point in this debate it may be appropriate to attempt a revision or a redrafting of the Treaties to reflect the concerns and lessons of the 1970s. That time is not yet because no consensus as to the form such a new Treaty should take is yet in sight. But it is in all our interests that the discussion should be steered in such a direction that, if and when a new Treaty seems appropriate, the drafters will be able to start work with the same background of consensus as guided their predecessors who drafted the Treaties of Paris and Rome.

What does this mean in concrete terms? It means, first, that the Commission itself should have a vision of the future which is more than a set of platitudes and a linear projection of the harmonisation process. In other words, the Commission should have a central planning function. That is something which has hitherto been rather conspicuously lacking.

Second, it means that the Commission must move away from the adversary posture *vis-à-vis* national governments to one of co-operation. For if a new mandate for the next stage of European integration is to evolve it is unlikely to be devised totally in Brussels. The national governments as well as the great sectional interests will have to be involved in the debate if the conclusions are to be meaningful and acceptable.

In fact, since 1973 there has been one potentially vital institutional innovation in the European Community. This is the growing practice of regular discussions — typically three times a year — between the heads of government of the Nine. This institution — misleadingly called the "European Council", not to be confused with the Council of Ministers — is the forum where the key decisions on European policy are in fact taken. It is the real seat of power in the Community. It has no formal status, it is not mentioned in any of the founding treaties of the Community, it has no official links with any of the other institutions. Its meetings are private, its decisions may or may not be published. Clearly the issues it discusses are those which are currently of major concern for the individual Community countries and thus for the Community as a whole. On the evidence to date it has succeeded in grappling with the appalling economic problems of the E.E.C. countries in a rather effective, pragmatic way. The practice of informal co-ordination of national economic policies, in contrast to the ineffective formal co-ordination of Economic and Monetary Union, does seem to have worked quite well at the level of the European Council. This is because the members have recognised that their countries have different immediate priorities and problems, different degrees of strength, different opportunities. Thus what has emerged is a flexible set of national policies in which each country discusses its policy with the others and   tries to ensure that in dealing with its internal problems it does not harm the interests of others. It is a policy of gradual convergence based on a recognition of differences and a general "good-neighbour" attitude of mutual assistance.

This is of course far removed from the more rigid formulae of the Treaty of Rome. But if the Commission is to continue to play a major role in the "making of Europe" it can hardly afford to ignore or stand aside from this development. It would clearly be desirable if the Commission could influence the discussions of the European Council by providing a secretariat and a follow-up mechanism, to ensure that the rather general pronouncements made by heads of government, who are short of time and have many other preoccupations, are translated into concrete actions at European level. In this way, by acting as a kind of European secretariat, the Commission could hopefully re-insert itself into the centre of the European debate, and dilute the heady wines of nationalism which could otherwise distort the integration process.

The establishment of close links between the Commission and the European Council would be one step in the reform of the European institutions. There are of course others. One of the most defective of these institutions at present is the Council of Ministers. Not only does the Council tend to deal with E.E.C. issues from the narrow point of arbitrage between conflicting national interests, rather than from a general vision of what is the European interest, it has also become very dilatory in taking any decisions at all; and when it does take decisions they are often mutually contradictory. This is because there is in fact *no* single Council of Ministers. There are meetings of particular groups of ministers concerned with a sectional interest — ministers of finance, or agriculture, or employment for example. There is no effective mechanism for ensuring that their decisions are co-ordinated. Thus ministers of agriculture can take decisions on farm prices which are not at all in accordance with decisions on the Community budget taken by the finance ministers.

It would therefore be highly desirable if there were to be a regular Council of Ministers from the Nine concerned with co-ordinating all aspects of European policy — ministers who would of course be joined from time to time by their specialist colleagues to discuss particular issues. The evolution of the European Council could well give a fillip to the establishment of such a body, which could both prepare European

Council meetings (with the assistance of the Commission), and carry on the business of Europe between European Council meetings. It would also be an important function of this revamped Council to discuss with the Commission its budget — not in the present patchwork form under which the Commission has in effect no control over the three-quarters of its budget which derives from the common agricultural policy; but in a more sensible form in which the Commission is required to spell out how it thinks its budget should be divided between the various priority areas, and why — so that for the first time in the story of the E.E.C., budgets would reflect and exemplify decisions on policies.

If the Commission is to work more closely with the ministers and officials of the national governments, how is the voice of Europe to be expressed? This is the role which has always been seen for the European Assembly or Parliament. It is in the Parliament that hitherto the authentic voice of European idealism has been most typically heard. The Parliament and the Council represent the two poles between which the Commission should balance itself. On the one hand, the Council represents the voice of power of those who have the ultimate authority of decision-making in Europe. But the Parliament represents the voice of European democratic authority — of those who are elected to speak, not for the nations, but for Europe. It is to the Parliament that the Commission is required to report. It is the Parliament, and the Parliament alone, which has the authority — so far never used — to dismiss the Commission. A President of the Commission who can command the support of the European Parliament is well placed to argue with authority if need be against the heads of government.

Up to now the two poles have been of markedly unequal strength. Not only does the Parliament lack the power of making laws; it is in fact merely a consultative body. Its members are not even directly elected. They are seconded on a part-time basis from their national legislatures. But this will shortly change. By a decision taken in the European Council in 1975, members of the European Parliament are supposed to be chosen by direct elections in all the nine countries by mid-1978. It is doubtful if this timetable can be fully adhered to. But in any event within a few years the great majority of members of the European Parliament will be full-time representatives directly elected to the job by constituents in their native countries.

This of itself will have a number of effects which will profoundly influence the constitutional map of Europe. First, it will give the Parliament a moral authority it has hitherto lacked. Second, it will probably make it less "European" and more subject to national pressures than in the past; for European M.P.s will now be subject to re-election by national constituencies who will be at least as much concerned with how their member is looking after their interests than with the overall development of the Community. The new European Parliament may be a little disillusioning for European idealists. But it is only by the direct interplay between European and sectional or grassroots interests that the Community can acquire reality in the minds of all its peoples.

A third effect of the reform will be to create a group of European parliamentarians who will initially have more time and energy than work to satisfy them. Full-time M.P.s will be much less ready than the present part-timers to be fobbed off with the consultative role which is all that the Parliament has — or will have, even after direct elections. It is a fact which has been little remarked on, for fear of the hornets' nest which could be stirred up on this issue, that after direct elections it is not envisaged that the Parliament will have any more powers than it has today.

But this is surely an untenable situation. As soon as a directly elected Parliament is in session its members are likely to start demanding the kind of powers which a normal democratic parliament has — the power to pass legislation, to call the executive to account and to control expenditure. This is a kind of constitutional issue with which the British are familiar. We fought a civil war over it three centuries ago. It is this issue which could well come to dominate the political scene in the E.E.C. in the years immediately after 1978.

Of course the issue is an extremely complex one. Which is the "executive" in this context? The Commission is the executive body corresponding to the Parliament. But, as we have seen, it is not the ultimate repository of power in the Community. What will be the relation between the Parliament and the European Council or the Council of Ministers? It would be desirable if these, too, were asked to report from time to time to the European Parliament. But if they did so would this be seen as infringing the prerogatives of the national legislatures?

The same question arises in the case of legislation. Ultimately, Community law has to be sanctioned by the national legislatures of the member-States since it is they who will have to enforce it. So how is a law-making function for the European Parliament to be reconciled with the same functions for the nine national parliaments? A possible long-term solution might be for the European Parliament to replace the second chambers in all the member-States, so that all those aspects of national legislation which had a European dimension would need to be discussed and approved by the European Parliament. But the day when such a proposal is regarded as practical politics may still be a little way off.

One body which will have to reconsider its role in relation to the evolution of the Parliament is the Economic and Social Committee, or "Ecosoc". Ecosoc was brought into being as a consultative body to represent the interests at European level of the "social partners" — the employers, the trade unions and a heterogeneous "third group" embracing consumers and certain special interests. It has not been conspicuously successful. For one thing it is excessively large and its procedures are slow and cumbersome. Second, its consultative functions at present exactly duplicate those of the Parliament, which has more prestige. Third, over the years the social partners have found more direct channels of access to the Commission and Council. First the unions and employers, and now the consumers, too, have established consultative committees and other direct links which give them better access to Community decision-making than the unwieldy Ecosoc. The Standing Committee on Employment is in many ways a break-away of Groups One and Two of Ecosoc, leaving Group Three out in the cold.

So Ecosoc has to discover a distinctive role for itself which does not duplicate that of other consultative groups. It would be ironic if the spread of social partner consultation led to the demise or decay of the main institution at Community level for such consultation. And in fact there are at least two specific functions which are not being effectively exercised in the present Community structure, which a suitably revamped Ecosoc would be well equipped to do.

One is the very detailed, tedious but essential role of reviewing and analysing in depth the implications of particular Commission proposals. Parliament itself is unlikely to carry out such a scrutiny with the thoroughness that a body bringing together employer, worker and consumer interests can bring to bear. National governments tend to study them from the narrow viewpoint of national interest, and then often superficially. Yet it is quite clear that proposals made by officials in Brussels can often have very far-reaching effects which are not foreseen, simply because of the complexities of national laws or practices which may simply not be understood at Community level. So an independent, expert review body is absolutely essential, and this Ecosoc is well geared to provide.

The second needed function is perhaps at the other extreme of the spectrum. Europe badly needs a body of independent experts whose job is to look into the future, to chart a possible course of long-term integration, to think beyond the policies and programmes of the next few years to the issues and challenges which lie ahead. The Commission, as we have seen, has not done this. Like all political bodies it tends to be dominated by short-term considerations. It is true that the study commissioned from the expert group entitled "Europe Plus Thirty", which was published in 1976, proposed a long-term "think-tank" capability linked to the Commission itself. This may or may not come to pass. Whether it does or not, it remains the case that the Commission needs its own planning capability; but that there is also a case for an independent body brooding continuously on the long-term problems and perspectives from the point of view of the peoples of Europe. This is a role which, in my view, Ecosoc should consider trying to fulfil.

We can envisage, then, a period of constitutional ferment over the next few years in the European Community as each of the *dramatis personae* seeks to establish a new role for itself. If all goes well we may expect to see a Commission which is working more closely with a European Council, on the one hand (and with a better-structured Council of Ministers which will be directly servicing the European Council), and with a more high-powered and demanding Parliament, on the other. Such a role offers considerable opportunities to the Commission provided the President is able to get a better control over the programmes and the public expressions of his colleagues than has been the case up to now. The President of the Commission is uniquely entitled to articulate the voice of "Europe" on the great issues of the day. He has the stature, the independence of national interests and the public platform afforded by the Parliament. But if the voice of Europe is expressed in different, discordant tones by thirteen different Commissioners, the effect tends to be a bit muffled; and that is what has tended to happen in the past. Also, to carry credibility the Commission has to be seen to have a coherent programme — a programme which is costed and budgeted, which reflects priorities which carry general acceptance, which is plainly relevant to the major issues of contemporary concern. Without this the Commission can be too easily bypassed and brushed aside as a dogmatic irrelevance.

It remains to be seen whether, in the next few decisive years, the Community institutions will successfully adapt to the needs of the day, and thus lay the groundwork for the much-needed regeneration of the E.E.C. — or whether we shall continue to see the erosion of the centre and the reversion of power to the governments of the member-States, who will settle issues between them on the basis of bilateral bargains and accommodations, without any central convergent pressures or idealism. If things go in this direction, the role to be played by a European social policy in the evolution of the Community is bound to be a rather marginal one. For, as we have seen, those aspects of social policy which positively *have* to be articulated and developed at Community level are few and far between. Europe does not *have* to have a social policy, as, for example, she *has* to have a common agricultural policy and a competition policy if the present structure is to survive.

But if the present structure is not just to stand still but to move forward — if the Europe that we want is to be more than a club of friendly states accepting certain mutual obligations and certain minimal common rules — then *some* aspects of social policy are in my view essential, and certain others (to put it no higher) are highly convenient.

Which aspects of current Community social policy come into these two categories? In the first category — the absolutely essential elements — come questions of employment, migration and social justice. Without a positive policy on employment the process of economic integration is unlikely to continue without interruption. If there is to be a European employment policy it has to concern itself with questions of immigration and of regional development as well as of issues of industrial structure. Thus social policy has to be linked not only with regional policy but also with industrial policy. If there is to be a manpower policy for the Community, it has to have as one of its elements a clear understanding of likely trends in different industrial sectors and contingency plans to cope with the problem areas.

I have argued in this book that a viable solution to the unemployment problems confronting Europe requires the kind of tripartite planning system — involving ministers concerned with economic policy as well as employment ministers, trade unions and employers — that the United Kingdom has developed through the N.E.D.C. structure, both at national and at sector level. The same kind of tripartite approach is needed if Europe is to find a viable solution to the other great social and economic evil of the day — inflation. Here again a prerequisite for effective action, at Community as at national level, is participation between governments and social partners.

Unless the Community can be seen to be tackling the twin dragons of employment and inflation, the political will to accept the disciplines of the Common Market and to progress with the creation of a united Europe is unlikely to be long maintained. The vision of the 1972 summit communiqué was not wrong. The real issues are still the ones then posed. But the realisation of the objectives has proved more difficult, the enthusiasm to do so more fickle, than was then thought. And the Community institutions have contributed to the squandering of precious goodwill by dissipating their efforts in too many directions.

A basic requirement, therefore, for Europe in the years ahead is an economic - social - industrial strategy for economic regeneration and development, full employment, reduction of inflation and better distribution of resources to be worked out in partnership between governments, social partners and Commission. This will be immensely difficult; some will say it is impossibly ambitious. But unless we try it is hardly worth talking about a European social policy at all since all other issues are in a real sense peripheral.

Put this way, of course, social policy ceases to be a separate, self-contained area of activity — as it has always tended to be regarded in Brussels — and becomes instead an integrated part of overall strategy, influenced by and influencing other policies. This too is crucial. The "ghetto mentality" which has afflicted those concerned with Community social policy in the past must go. Social policy is too central to our concerns for that approach to be tolerable.

But, if these issues are to be the core of the next stage of Europe's social policy, there are other elements which also have a part to play. I leave on one side here — not because they are unimportant but because they have already been discussed and are in a sense less controversial — the on-going commitments which arise from the Treaty or from other Community programmes or decisions. I refer here to continuing work on the programmes for women, migrants, environmental control, health and safety, social security harmonisation, etc.

A more important element, in the long run, is that which I would term the "convenient" rather than the "essential" part of social policy — the "soft" as opposed to the "hard" element, as some would prefer to call it. By that I mean the complex of issues which are not essential to Europe's economic survival nor to the achievement of the terms of the Rome Treaty, but which nevertheless concern the kind of society which the Community will be and the quality of life in it; issues which do not involve conflicting national interests, where policies of convergence are therefore both feasible and acceptable. Typically, these are issues where each member-State has identified common problems which can more readily be solved by united action than by separate and isolated endeavours.

Many such issues in the social field have been identified in the last few years, and it has been one of the arguments in this book that the catalytic role which the Commission has been able to play in their solution has been one of the underestimated successes of European policy. Examples of this role have been the moves to co-ordinate national policies in the field of employment, social protection, public health research, re-habilitation of the disabled, vocational training, anti-poverty pro-grammes, work humanisation and the like. The more that E.E.C. members come to pool their thinking and their approaches to issues of this kind, the more the habit of convergence will grow and the more the E.E.C. will come to resemble a real Community. I have no doubt that this habit of pragmatic co-ordination — exemplified at the highest level by the work of the European Council — will grow, given the will, and that from it can be developed a more broadly based conception of the European Community than that set out in the Rome Treaty.

This is not in any sense to denigrate the Treaty. The Common Market remains the base from which European integration has to grow, and the first requirement is to make sure that that base remains strong and inviolate. It has been argued in this book that unless economic integration is accompanied by social policies to ensure jobs, social justice and an acceptable allocation of resources, the base could be threatened by a combination of sectional or national autarkic pressures and apathy. So that is the first task of European social policy — to humanise the process of economic growth and integration. But the evolution of a European Community is not just an economic process. It is also a question of achieving convergent approaches to common problems designed to ensure that the shape and nature of the Community corresponds to what its citizens would wish; and here, too, a European social policy has a major role to play.

To protect and strengthen what has been achieved and to improve the future quality of European life: these must be the guidelines of social policy in the E.E.C. Both rest on a judgement which I am convinced history will endorse; a judgement that the ultimate sanction for the future European Community of nations — whatever constitutional form that Community may eventually take — will be found to rest, not in the clauses of the Rome Treaty, but in the hearts and minds of our peoples, who have to decide whether or not such a Community has enough value to justify a continued political commitment to unity. That is the battle which still has to be won. Social policy alone cannot decide it, but without the added dimension of social policy no combination of other measures can achieve success.

Index